Florida

MAPPING THE SUNSHINE STATE THROUGH HISTORY

Detail from map on pages 12 and 13

Florida

MAPPING THE SUNSHINE STATE THROUGH HISTORY

Rare and Unusual Maps from the Library of Congress

Vincent Virga

and E. Lynne Wright

Guilford, Connecticut

To buy books in quantity for corporate use
or incentives, call **(800) 962-0973**
or e-mail **premiums@GlobePequot.com**.

Text design: Sheryl P. Kober
Project editor: Julie Marsh
Layout artist: Casey Shain

Library of Congress Cataloging-in-Publication Data

Virga, Vincent.
  Florida, mapping the sunshine state through history : rare and unusual maps from the
Library of Congress.
    p. cm.
  ISBN 978-0-7627-6010-7
  1. Historical geography—Florida—Maps. I. Wright, E. Lynne, 1932- II. Title.
  G1315 .V6 2011
  911'.759—dc22
                                                                    2010022990

Printed in China
10 9 8 7 6 5 4 3 2 1

Contents

FLORIDA'S ANCIENT BEDROCK HAS REVEALED THAT the "Sunshine State" was once part of northwest Africa. Geologists call the Florida Plateau "exotic terrain." So what else is new? My northern-bred imagination equates Florida with tropical flora and fauna, Technicolor warmth, and an eternally enticing Atlantic coastline where, during the last ice age, myriad creatures, including saber-toothed cats, migrated to escape the frigid north. Assisted by our eternally enticing maps, E. Lynne Wright adeptly reveals why one of the youngest regions in the continental United States has the longest recorded history. Spain's Ponce de León encounters two hundred thousand Native Americans in 1513, and the saga continues under the steward- ship of England and France before self-realization is achieved and Florida becomes a bastion of many well-earned American dreams.

Living on planet Earth has always raised cer- tain questions from those of us so inclined. Of course, the most obvious one is: Where am I? Well, as Virginia Woolf sagely noted in her diary, writ- ing things down makes them more real; this may have been a motivating factor for the Old Stone Age artists who invented the language of signs on the walls of their caves in southern France and northern Spain eleven thousand to thirty- seven thousand years ago. Picasso reportedly said,

"They've invented everything," which includes the very concept of an image.

A map is an image. It makes the world more real for us and uses signs to create an essential sense of place in our imagination. (Early examples of such signs are the petroglyphic maps that were inscribed in the late Iron Age on boulders high in the Valcamonica region of northern Italy.) Car- tographic imaginings not only locate us on this earth but also help us invent our personal and social identities since maps embody our social order. Like the movies, maps helped create our national identity—though cinema had a vastly wider audience—and this encyclopedic series of books aims to make manifest the changing social order that invented the United States, which is why it embraces all fifty states.

Each is a precious link in the chain of events that is the history of our "great experiment," the first enduring federal government ingeniously deriving its just powers—as John Adams pro- posed—from the consent of the governed. Each state has a physical presence that holds a unique place in any representation of our republic in maps. To see each one rise from the body of the conti- nent conjures Thomas Paine's excitement over the resourcefulness, the fecundity, the creative energy of our Enlightenment philosopher-founders: "We are brought at once to the point of seeing government begin, as if we had lived in the beginning of time." Just as the creators systemized not only laws but also rights in our constitution, so our maps show how their collective memory inspired the body politic to organize, codify, classify all of Nature to do their bidding with passionate preferences state by state. For they knew, as did Alexander Pope:

> All are but parts of one
> stupendous Whole
> Whose body Nature is,
> and God the soul.

And aided by the way maps under interrogation often evoke both time and space, we editors and historians have linked the reflective historical overviews of our nation's genesis to the seduction of place embedded in the art and science of cartography.

On October 9, 1492, after sailing westward for four weeks in an incomprehensibly vast and unknown sea, an anxious Christopher Columbus spotted an unidentified flock of migrating birds flying south and signifying land—"Tierra! Tierra!" Changing course to align his ships with this overhead harbinger of salvation, he avoided being drawn into the northern-flowing Gulf Stream, which was waiting to be charted by Ben Franklin around the time our eagle became America as art. And so, on October 11, Columbus encountered the salubrious southern end of San Salvador. Instead of somewhere in the future New England, he came up the lee of the island's west coast to an easy and safe anchorage.

Lacking maps of the beachfront property before his eyes, he assumed himself in Asia because in his imagination there were only three parts to the known world: Europe, Asia, and Africa. To the day he died, Columbus doubted he had come upon a fourth part, even though Europeans had already begun appropriating through the agency of maps what to them was a New World, a new continent. Perhaps the greatest visual statement of the general confusion that rocked the Old World as word spread of Columbus's interrupted journey to Asia is the Ruysch map of 1507 (see page viii). Here we see our nascent home inserted into the template created in the second century by Ptolemy, a mathematician, astrologer, and geographer of the Greco-Roman known world, the *oikoumene.*

This map changed my life. It opened my eyes to the power of a true cultural landscape. It taught me that I must always *look* at what I *see* on a map, focusing my attention on why the map was made, not who made it, when or where it was made, but *why.* The Ruysch map was made to circulate the current news. It is a quiet, meditative moment in a very busy, noisy time. It is life on the cusp of a new order. And the new order is what Henry Steele Commager christened the "utopian romance" that is America. No longer were maps merely mirrors of nature for me. No longer were the old ones "incorrect" and ignorant of the "truth." No longer did they exist simply to orient me in the practical world. The Ruysch map is reality circa 1507! It is a time machine. It makes the invisible past visible. Blessedly free of impossible abstractions and idealized virtues, it is undeniably my sort of primary historical document.

The same year, 1507, the Waldseemüller map appeared (see page ix). It is yet another reality and one very close to the one we hold dear. There we Americans are named for the first time. And there we sit, an independent continent with oceans on

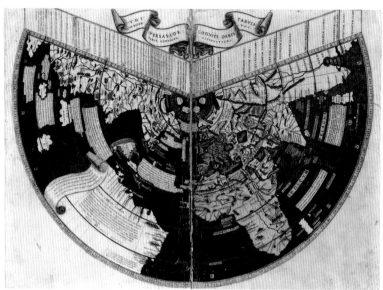
Ruysch map, 1507

who reveres maps as storytellers, am both a word person and a person who can think in pictures. This is the modus operandi of a mapmaker recording the world in images for the visually literate. For a traditional historian, maps are merely archival devices dealing with scientific accuracy. They cannot "see" a map as a first-person, visual narrative crammed with very particular insights to the process of social history. However, the true nature of maps as a key player in the history of the human imagination is a cornerstone of our series.

both sides of us, six years *before* Balboa supposedly discovered "the other sea." There are few maps as mysterious for cartographic scholars as Waldseemüller's masterpiece. Where did all that news come from? For our purposes it is sufficient to say to the world's visual imagination, "Welcome to us Americans in all our cartographic splendor!"

Throughout my academic life, maps were never offered to me as primary historical documents. When I became a picture editor, I learned, to my amazement, that most book editors are logocentric, or "word people." (And thank God! If they weren't, I wouldn't have my career.) Along with most historians and academics, they make their livelihood working with words and ideas. The fact of my being an "author" makes me a word person, too, of course.

But I store information visually, as does a map. (If I ask myself where my keys are, I "see" them in my mind's eye; I don't inform myself of their whereabouts in words.) So I, like everyone

The very title of this volume, *Florida: Mapping the Sunshine State through History*, makes it clear that this series has a specific agenda, as does each map. It aims to thrust us all into a new intimacy with the American experience by detailing the creative process of our nation in motion through time and space via word *and* image. It grows from the relatively recent shift in consciousness about the physical, mental, and spiritual relevance of maps in our understanding of our lives on Earth. Just as each state is an integral part of the larger United States, "Where are we?" is a piece of the larger puzzle called "Who are we?"

The Library of Congress was founded in 1800 with 740 volumes and three maps. It has grown into the world's largest library and is known as "America's Memory." For me, its vast visual holdings made by those who helped build this nation make the Library the eyes of our

Waldseemüller map, 1507

nation as well. There are nearly five million maps in the Geography and Map Division. We have linked our series with that great collection in the hopes that its astonishing breadth will inspire us in our efforts to strike Lincoln's "mystic chords of memory" and create living history.

On January 25, 1786, Thomas Jefferson wrote to Archibald Stuart, "Our confederacy must be viewed as the nest from which all America, North and South, is to be peopled." This is a man who could not live without books. This is a man who drew maps. This is a politician who in spite of his abhorrence of slavery and his respect for Native Americans took pragmatic rather than principled positions when confronted by both "issues." Nonetheless, his bold vision of an expanded American universe informs our current enterprise. There is no denying that the story of the United States has a dark side. What

makes the American narrative unique is the ability we have displayed time and again to remedy our mistakes, to adjust to changing circumstances, to debate, and then move on in new directions that seem better for all.

For Jefferson, whose library was the basis for the current Library of Congress after the British burned the first one during the War of 1812, and for his contemporaries, the doctrine of progress was a keystone of the Enlightenment. The maps in our books are reports on America, and all of their political programs are manifestations of progress. Our starting fresh, free of Old World hierarchies, class attitudes, and the errors of tradition, is wedded to our geographical isolation and its immunity from the endless internal European wars devastating humanity, which justify Jefferson's confessing, "I like the dreams of the future better than the history of the past." But, as the historian Michael Kammen explains, "For much of our history we have been present-minded; yet a usable past has been needed to give shape and substance to national identity." Historical maps keep the past warm with life and immediately around us. They encourage critical inquiry, curiosity, and qualms.

For me, this series of books celebrating each of our states is not about the delineation of property rights. It is a depiction of the pursuit of happiness, which is listed as one of our natural rights in the 1776 Declaration of Independence. (Thirteen years later, when the French revolutionaries drafted a Declaration of the Rights of Man, they included "property rights," and Jefferson unsuccessfully urged them to substitute "pursuit of happiness" for "property.") Jefferson also believed, "The Earth belongs always to the living generation." I believe these books depict what each succeeding generation in its pursuit of happiness accomplished on this portion of the Earth known as the United States. If America is a matter of an idea, then maps are an image of that idea.

I also fervently believe these books will show the states linked in the same way Lincoln saw the statement that all men are created equal as "the electric cord in that Declaration that links the hearts of patriotic and liberty-loving men together, that will link those patriotic hearts as long as the love of freedom exists in the minds of men throughout the world."

VINCENT VIRGA
WASHINGTON, D.C.
2010

Introduction

FLORIDA CLAIMS A SIZABLE SHORELINE ON THE Atlantic Ocean and the Gulf of Mexico, plus various bays, lagoons, 12,000 miles of rivers, 7,700 large lakes, 600 springs, 660 miles of beaches, not to mention prairies, good weather, and sunshine. So, is there anything this odd-shaped peninsula doesn't have to brag about? Well, because the highest point in the entire state is just 345 feet above sea level, mountain climbers will most likely not be attracted to the Sunshine State. But, for thousands of years, other human beings have found countless reasons to journey to the Land of Flowers, all the way back to when they crossed over the bridge of ice from Siberia to Alaska, then continued south on the continent, eon after eon. Water was no small part of Florida's allure.

Florida's land measures 792 miles from Pensacola, at the western point, to Key West, the farthest southern island in the Keys. With the stretch of such a distance, it's not surprising that variation exists not only in Flrida's geography, but also in her people and her culture. Accidentally discovered by Ponce de León in 1513, Florida has the longest documented history of any state in the United States. During that time, Florida was shaped and reshaped by four countries, Spain, England, France, and finally, the United States.

Included among the many rivers important to Florida life are two that are unique and are less than forty miles apart. The Everglades, that strange River of Grass made famous by writer and environmentalist Marjory Stoneman Douglas, flows south, supplies water for millions of people, plants, and animals, and helps to determine the climate as well as the livelihood of commercial fishermen and related workers.

The other one-of-a-kind river, the Gulf Stream, a river in the ocean, flows north along the eastern Florida coast, moving approximately one hundred billion tons of water past Miami at the rate of two to five miles per hour, affecting lives and climate in countless ways. Although Ponce de León discovered the Gulf Stream, Ben Franklin gets credit for naming it.

Florida's western border is defined by the Perdido River. A short river, just sixty miles long, it forms the shared boundary between Florida and Alabama and was formerly the boundary between Spain's colony of Florida and France's colony of Louisiana.

The St. Johns River on Florida's east coast flows north, parallel to the shore, for 310 miles, the state's longest river. A vital travel artery in the early years, it was replaced in time by railroads, then by the highway Interstate 95. At present, environmentalists are working hard to preserve the beauty of the St. Johns River.

The distance from St. Augustine in the east to Pensacola at the western end of the state measures 386 miles. No waterways flow between the two cities, and in territorial days before there were roadways, that formidable distance required fifty-nine days of travel for delegates at either end to meet and conduct the business of Florida's government at the other end. At the second legislative session, Tallahassee, centrally located, was chosen to be the capital.

Farther east and closer to the middle of the state, just below Gainesville, lies a broad area of coarse grasses and scattered trees, a basin that resulted when sinkholes formed close to each other, eventually connecting to become a great shallow bowl named Paynes Prairie. Periodically, the hole that drains the prairie becomes clogged and the basin floods. In the 1800s, Paynes Prairie turned into Alachua Lake and was deep enough for boats to cross for a few years before it drained again and the lake became a prairie once more.

Farther south, between Tampa and Orlando, stretches the Green Swamp, an oasis of wetlands, the state's second largest after the Everglades. Within this 560,000-acre swamp, is the highest point of the Florida Aquifer, which provides water to many springs, five major rivers, and countless lakes, ponds, and streams. Disney World lies nearby in the east, and as development expands from Tampa on the west, the natural plants and trees that support the 330 species of wildlife residing in the Green Swamp are of great concern.

Disney World has been a blessing and a curse to the Orlando area. Originally a citrus-producing region that was mostly wetlands, the area exploded with population and development

when the resort opened in 1971. Best known primarily for the Disney World, Universal, and Sea-World resorts, Orlando now boasts an expanding technology industry, developing film and television operations, other high-tech manufacturing and engineering facilities, and the second-busiest airport in the state after Miami. Orlando International Airport occupies the land that was formerly the McCoy Air Force Base, the base for U-2 reconnaissance aircraft during the Cuban Missile Crisis in 1962.

To the east and slightly south, the land juts into the ocean forming a cape, prone to such occasional ferocious tides and winds that an Englishman in the sixteenth century said of it, "No ship escapeth which cometh thither." He was referring to Cape Canaveral, which even the Seminoles, when they were being badgered to leave Florida, passed on before taking refuge in the Everglades. Except for a few small settlements, the area remained mostly uninhabited until the United States bought land there to build the Banana River Naval Air Station during World War II. Deserted at the war's end, interest in the relatively isolated area intensified as the government became increasingly concerned with the success German rockets had demonstrated against England during the war. Following the launch of Sputnik in 1957 by the Communist Soviet Union, U.S. president Dwight D. Eisenhower signed a law creating NASA, the National Aeronautics and Space Administration. The agency grew with breathtaking speed, landed men on the moon, built the tallest one-story building in the world, and made discoveries that have unlocked countless secrets and turned science fiction into science fact.

The coastal settlements along the east coast below the Cape, self-described as being more like "old Florida," are known as the Treasure Coast, named for the pieces of treasure that wash up after storms. As a result of the many shipwrecks that have occurred in the area from earliest times to the present, folks still scan the beach with metal detectors and salvage crews work the waters with occasional spectacular success.

As the beaches stretch farther south along the coast, housing developments crowd closer together, high-rise condos appear with increasing frequency, and towns and cities run into one another to form a giant seaside megalopolis, running from Palm Beach, through Fort Lauderdale, on down to Miami, encompassing what has come to be known as the Gold Coast. A few miles inland, 730 square miles of Lake Okeechobee, the second-largest freshwater lake within the continental United States, lies at nearly the center of the state, connected to each coast by a canal.

Miami, the only major U.S. city founded by a woman, would be unrecognizable to Julia Tuttle today. Closer to the Caribbean than to the capital at Tallahassee, Miami-Dade County has morphed from a nearly uninhabitable wilderness infested with mosquitoes, snakes, and alligators into a city of gleaming skyscrapers and a population that speaks so many languages that a lost tourist can have a difficult time finding someone who can understand his questions.

The barrier islands that line the Gold Coast continue on to become the Florida Keys. U.S. Route 1, with mile 0 in Key West, runs up the East Coast all the way to the Canadian border. The subtropical climate of the Keys makes it seem more Caribbean than Floridian.

Back on the mainland, at the tip of the peninsula, is the southernmost edge of the Everglades, that famed River of Grass, which long ago covered most of the state from Orlando down to Florida Bay. With the Everglades described as "useless swampland" and as "useless as the deserts of Africa," the visionaries of the 1800s began a war on nature that converted a natural water management system into an ecological disaster, resulting in the Everglades being dammed, diverted, turned into a sewer, and reduced to half its original size. Conservationists were alarmed, but in 2000, in an unusual show of bipartisanship, the Everglades were blessed by Congress passing and President Bill Clinton signing a bill to authorize the biggest environmental restoration plan in history. Nearly everyone agreed, it was a start, but just that—a start.

The west coast of the state, beginning with Naples, running northward to Tarpon Springs, and including the Greater Tampa Bay area, is informally called the Florida Suncoast, famed for miles of fine sandy beaches. Sparsely settled and with little industry other than fishing before Henry Plant built his railway, the region grew rapidly after Vicente Martinez Ybor moved his cigar manufacturing facility from Key West to Tampa in the 1880s and others soon followed.

The Florida Panhandle is so far west, residents considered selling their lands to Alabama for $1 million after the Civil War. Now noted for its military bases, the Panhandle's white sandy beaches attract crowds of college students each year for spring break.

Florida enjoyed unprecedented growth after World War II. Life was easier for many people—better roads, accessible shopping, more conveniences. The problem was, it didn't stop. There were too many housing developments, too many cars, ugly strip malls everywhere, not to mention dire warnings about water quality, loss of wildlife habitat, etc., etc., etc. And Florida woke up, knowing she had a very big job to do.

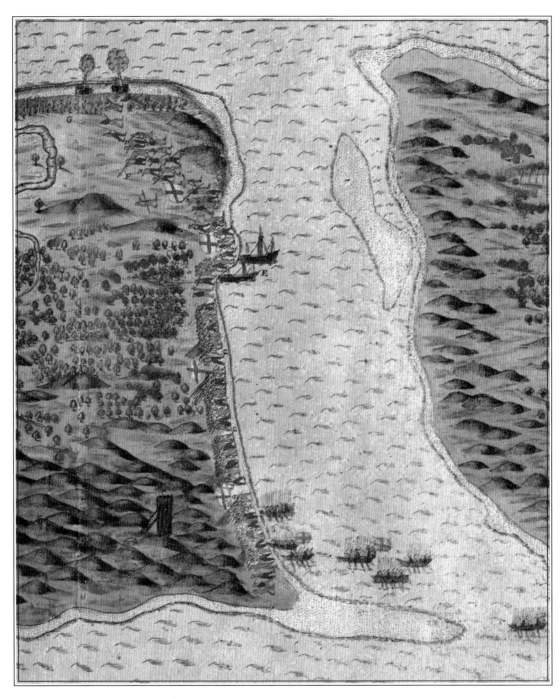

Detail from map on pages 14 and 15

First Encounters

In 1513, when Juan Ponce de León, a Spaniard, first landed near present-day Melbourne Beach, the recorded history of Florida began, long before that of any other state. The English settlement at Jamestown, Virginia, did not take place until 1607. The Pilgrims, familiar to all schoolchildren, did not land at Plymouth, Massachusetts, until 1620. By the time they arrived, St. Augustine was fifty-five years old; the others were the new kids on the block.

In actuality, Ponce de León did not even "discover" Florida. When he arrived, somewhere in the neighborhood of two hundred thousand Native Americans were living here. Prominent among the tribes that were here to greet the Spaniards were the Timucuan in north Florida and the Calusa, mostly in the south. Probably best known to Floridians today were the Seminoles. They actually were tribes that had broken off from the Creeks and, like so many present-day Floridians, had migrated here from another place, from Georgia or the Carolinas.

Ponce de León had accompanied Christopher Columbus on his second voyage to America when Puerto Rico was discovered. The king of Spain then appointed Ponce de León to be governor of Hispaniola and of Puerto Rico, so he remained on the island of Hispaniola, hoping to establish a settlement and find riches. That venture came to an ignominious end after Columbus died, when his son claimed all rights to his father's possessions, including the right to install his own people in chosen positions. As a result, Ponce de León lost his job.

He decided to pursue his own goals, make his own discoveries, and accordingly, set out with three ships, heading north until he reached what he thought was another island. It was most likely the area now called Melbourne Beach, and he named it *La Florida*, the Land of Flowers. Ponce de León and his men returned the seemingly friendly waves from Indians on shore, but when he and some of his men began to row ashore, they were greeted with a flurry of arrows and spears and forced to beat a hasty retreat. Ponce de León returned for another try in 1521, received a similar greeting, and this time he was wounded. Soon after retreating to Cuba, he died of his wounds. Although he never realized what he had actually discovered, Ponce de León is credited in history books as the discoverer of the Land of Flowers.

In 1528 another Spaniard, Pánfilo de

Narváez, and his men searched the southwest Florida coast for gold but were shipwrecked and lost their lives. Hernando de Soto, also Spanish, and his men were more successful, landing near the Tampa Bay area in 1539. They continued much farther and eventually discovered the Mississippi River before de Soto died there.

The vast stake Ponce de Léon claimed for Spain encompassed all the land from the southernmost point of Florida, north to the Chesapeake Bay, and west as far as the Mississippi River. Other Spanish explorers followed, looking not so much for territory to settle, but for the fabled riches they expected to find. During these expeditions, not only did the Spanish adventurers forcibly capture Indians to use as guides, but the diseases they spread to the natives, who had no resistance to them, quickly decimated large numbers of the native population.

Meanwhile in 1564, the French Huguenots, or French Protestants, established a settlement on the St. Johns River. Called Fort Caroline, the outpost lasted only a year before it was destroyed by Spanish forces under the command of Don Pedro Menéndez de Avilés, who named his base camp St. Augustine, the first permanent European settlement on the continent.

While Spain held Florida for two hundred years, England was establishing colonies to the north. In the 1580s Sir Francis Drake sailed from England with 2,300 men intending to capture Havana. After stops at Santo Domingo and Cartagena, he headed home, stopping only long enough to destroy the settlement at St. Augustine.

With the northern English colonies displaying an obvious interest in expansion, Spain became concerned, particularly since the Indians began to involve themselves in the growing fric-

tion. Adding to the animosity, slaves from English colonies were escaping to Florida, where Spanish law protected them. Some who joined the Seminoles became known as Black Seminoles.

Spain's power was slipping, but in 1672 she initiated the construction of a remarkable fort, Castillo de San Marcos, built entirely of coquina, a native shellrock. The fort took twenty-three years to complete, endured countless enemy attacks, and to this day, still stands guard over the city of St. Augustine.

Meanwhile, at the other end of the territory, Spain had not been forceful about protecting her interest in the Gulf Coast. When France showed signs of attempting to establish camp there, there was a sudden display of Spanish power, which convinced the French to speedily depart toward the west, where they established settlements in Louisiana.

When Britain captured Cuba in 1762, it was a territory of extreme importance to all of Spanish America. The island was held in such high regard that just one year later, Spain made a trade, exchanging the vast area of Florida for the small island of Cuba.

Florida was divided into two colonies during the nearly twenty years the English held it, East Florida and West Florida. They would remain the fourteenth and fifteenth colonies until Spanish armies marched into West Florida in 1779 during the Revolutionary War and the English were forced to depart.

During the English period, the Seminoles had mostly lived peaceably among them. After England surrendered control to Spain in 1781, it still burned in the memories of many whites that the Seminoles had helped the English, and the bitterness grew.

Some white settlers from the new United States rushed to Florida, hoping to take advantage of the Spanish land grants that were available. Other whites, without permission, simply moved onto desirable Seminole lands and set up their own farms. Still others looked for and captured slaves, whatever their color. The warnings issued by the Seminoles were ignored, and ferocious raids ensued. Tensions intensified, finally erupting into the First Seminole War, the first of three.

The secretary of war appointed Andrew Jackson to use whatever military means he felt necessary to resolve the situation. Old Hickory became a hero despite his abrasive personality and imperial manner, ruthlessly burning towns, wiping out settlements, destroying food and livestock, even hanging some Seminoles, and forcing others out of the territory. By May 1818 large numbers of Seminoles drifted farther south, among them, a future warrior named Osceola.

The advance of Jackson's forces into Florida was considered an act of war against Spain, which could no longer afford to pay for enough soldiers to patrol the borders of its colonial realm. Jackson's troops brazenly struck some Spanish properties, escalating the crisis.

In answer to Spain's protests, the United States offered and Spain accepted $5 million for the territory.

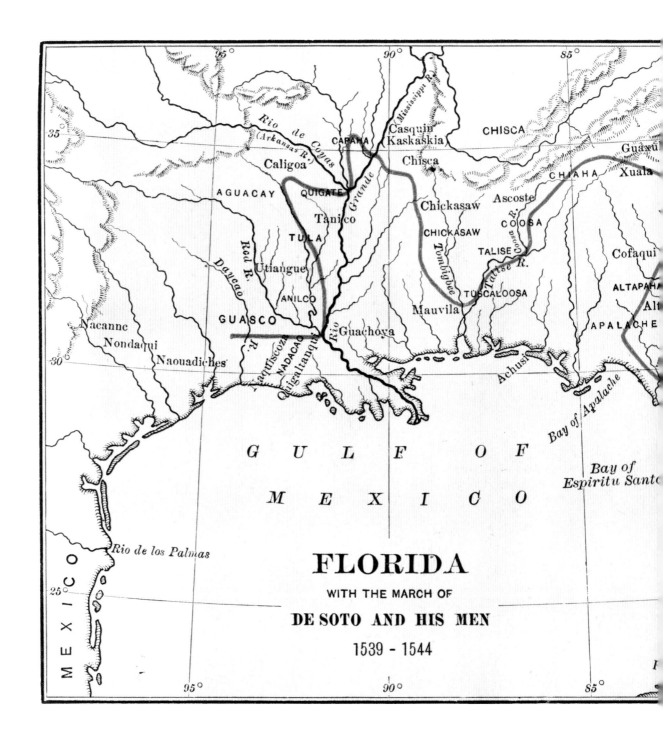

FLORIDA

WITH THE MARCH OF

DE SOTO AND HIS MEN

1539 - 1544

Florida with the march of de Soto and his men—
Bormay & Co. (1539–44)

A wealthy young man, Hernando de Soto left Spain with a squadron of ships in 1538 and landed on the west coast of Florida near Tampa Bay, in search of more riches and fame. He and his men marched through much of the present Southern states, all the way to the banks of the Mississippi River. As they traveled, de Soto's party unintentionally spread diseases to the natives, who had no immunity to them.

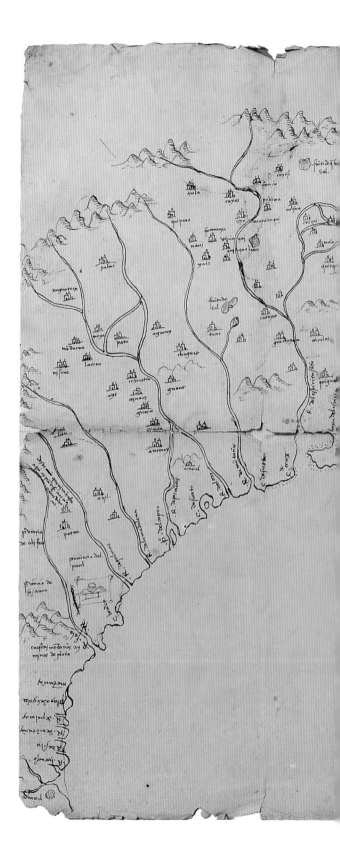

Mapa del Golfo y costa de la Nueva España, desde el Río de Panuco hasta el cabo de Santa Elena— Santa Cruz (1572?)

The map shows the coast from North Carolina's Cape Fear River, where de Soto and his group camped before they crossed the Great Smoky Mountains of Tennessee, then forged on to Pensacola, Arkansas, and Missouri. Some Indians at the settlement shown on the map were friendly, but not all were. De Soto was severely wounded by hostile natives, died of infection, and was buried at the mouth of the Arkansas River.

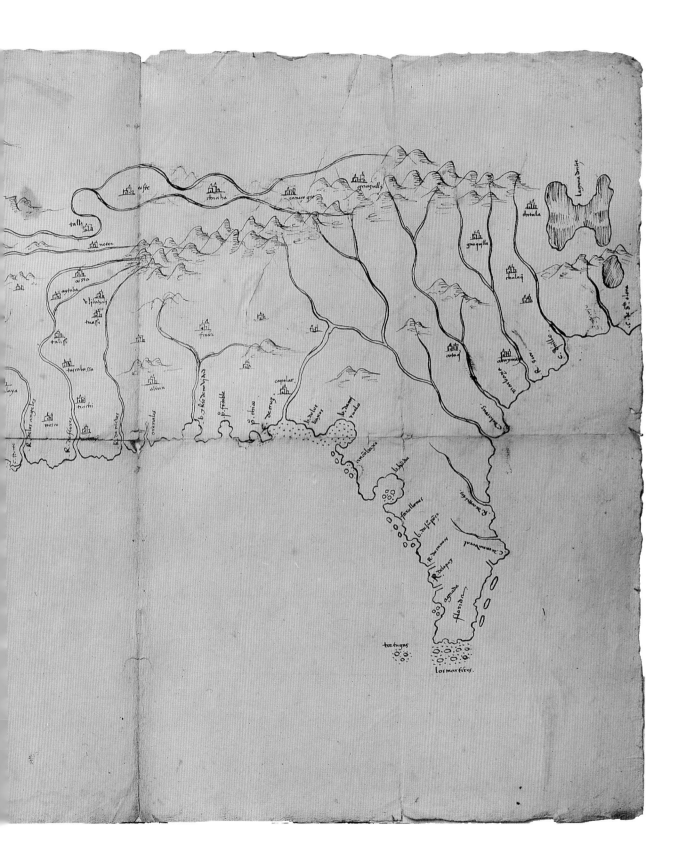

talli

auste

itnaha

caneo ga

gnagulli

laguna dulce

neter

dutala

costa

aytaba

gnagylla

b.hiahah

chalaq

tuaffe

finaz

taliffi

c. de s.te elena

tasralussa

aluca

capalar

costaq

abaynas

talaya

b.s.rio dematyhas

p.piguable

p.alma

derrug

R. los angelos

trachi

b.alos layos

cabalaços

mosn

b. de san nicolo

costabago

b.hinda

facallones

b.telayos

R. de mano

R. de matteos

R. de salguas

aguada

florida

tortugas

los martires.

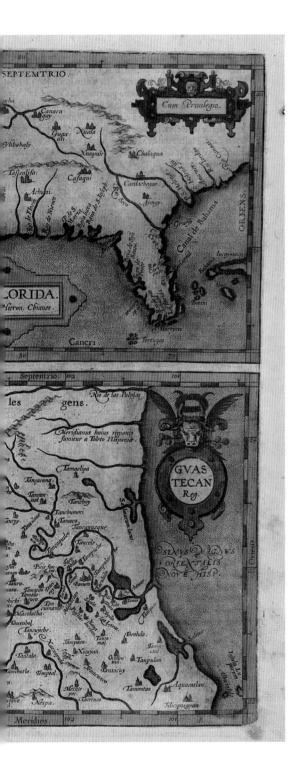

Peruuiae avriferæ regionis typus; Didaco Mendezio auctore.
La Florida; auctore Hieron. Chiaues. Guastecan reg.—
Ortelius (1584)

This map was regarded as an important work and is the most widely duplicated among early maps of this portion of North America. The extensive area of the southeastern part of the continent was all considered to be Florida at that time.

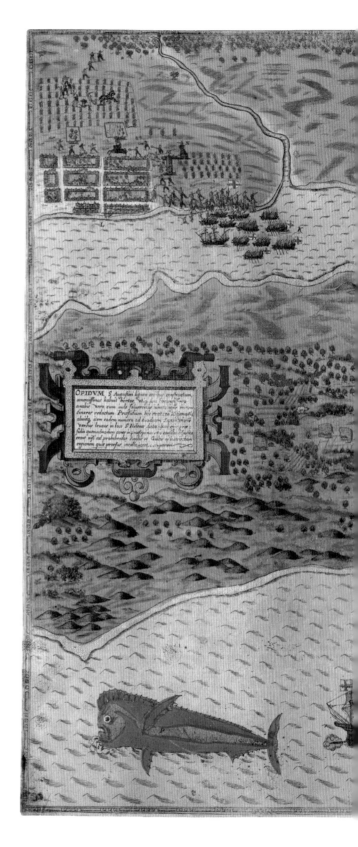

Map and views illustrating Sir Francis Drake's West Indian voyage—Boazio (1585–86)

Sir Frances Drake sailed from England in 1585 with a fleet of twenty ships in search of riches and intending to capture Havana. When illness decimated his crew, he felt pressured to return home, stopping at Santo Domingo on Hispaniola and Cartagena, Colombia. When, by chance, he spotted St. Augustine as he headed north, he paused there just long enough to destroy the small settlement.

S AVGVSTINI
pars est terra Floridæ
sub latitudine 30 grad
orum. Vero marime
humilior est, tan-
tanta et insu-
lofissima.

FLORIDA PROVINCIA

AB INDIGENIS DICTA IAQVAZA

Montes Apalatci, in quibus aurum, argentum & aes inueniuntur

Apalatci

In hoc lacu Indigena argenti grana inueniunt

Mexicani Sinus pars

Adeo magnus est hic lacus
ut ex una ripa conspici altera
non possit. Distat a Charles
fort 180 leucis.

Lacus & Insula Sarrope

CALOS

Insula dicta Testudines

Scopuli dicti Martyres

Hac maris pars plena est Insulis, scopulis, breuibus et puluinis valde insidiosis.

OCCIDENS

Havana

Cuba insula.

Guanaynarico

Insula Pinorii

Iardines scopuli, nauigantibus formidabiles.

S. Trinitatis

S. Io. Christi

Cuspis S. Antonij

Floridae Americae provinciae recens & exactissima descriptio auctorè Iacobo le Moyne cui cognomen de Morgues, qui Laudonierum, altera Gallorum in eam prouinciam nauigatione comitat est, atque adhibitis aliquot militibus ob pericula, regionis illius interiora & maritima diligentissimè lustrauit, & exactissimè dimensus est, obseruata etiam singulorum fluminum inter se distantia, ut ipsemet redux Carolo .IX. Galliarum regi, demonstrauit.—Le Moyne de Morgues (1591)

Jacques Le Moyne produced this map while he accompanied Laudonnière, who was trying to establish a French colony at the mouth of the St. Johns River, which the French called the River May. At the beginning of the river, Le Moyne depicts Lake George, believed at that time to be Florida's largest lake.

They reach Port Royal—Bry (1591)

French captain Jean Ribaut commanded an expedition to the New World in 1562. He installed a French claim with an impressive column of marble at the mouth of the St. Johns River, before he moved on north to Port Royal harbor and founded a colony protected by Charlesfort. The map, engraved by Theodor de Bry after a watercolor by Jackques LeMoyne, shows wildlife in the native habitat.

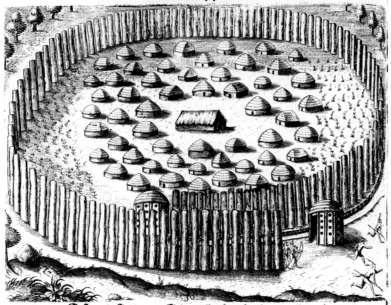

XXX.

Wie der Floridaner Stätte
erbauwet seyen.

S pflegen die Indianer jre Stätte auff diese weise zu bauwen. Wann sie einen Platz bey einer fürüber fliessenden Bach erwehlet haben/machen sie denselbigen/so viel es jhnen müglich ist/eben/vñ eine gar rondte Furche herumb/nachmals schlagen sie dicke vnd rondte Pfähle/zweyer Männer hoch/zusammen in die Erden/vnd da man in die Statt gehen sol/daselbst hin ziehen sie es rondt/vnnd schneckenweiß/zusammen/auff daß sie den Eingang der Statt desto enger machen/ vnd auff einmahl nicht mehr dann zween hindurch passiren können. Sie leyten auch die Bach zu demselbigen Ort hinzu. Vornen am Eingang pflegen sie ein kleines rondtes Häußlein zu bauwen/ darnach noch ein anders / da sich dieser Ort endet / vnd sind diese beyde Häuser rondt herumb voll Ritz vnd Löcher/ vnd also nach Gelegenheyt deß Lands/gar herrlich gebauwet. In diese Häuser werden solche Leute zu Hütern gesetzt/welche die Fußstapffen der Feinde von ferrne riechen können. Daß so baldt sie die Fußstapffen durch jre Naßlöcher vernommen/ gehen sie jnen entgegen / Vnd wann sie die Feinde antreffen / fangen sie als baldt an mit heller Stimm zu schreyen/ wann dann die Einwohner dieses Geschrey erhören / lauffen sie in Eile / mit Bogen/Pfeilen vnd Spiessen bewapnet/ die Statt zubeschützen/zusammen. Des Königs Hauß stehet mitten in der Statt / vnd von wegen der Sonnen Hitze ein wenig in die Erden hinein gebauwet / vmb dieses herumb stehen die Häuser deren vom Adel / mit Palmen zweygen sein dünn gedecket / Dann sie gebrauchen sich derselbigen nur neun Monat/ die andern drey Monat bringen sie (wie gesagt) in den Wälden zu / auß welchen/wann sie darnach wider kommen / ziehen sie widerumb in diese jhre Häuser. Wann sie aber sehen / daß sie durch jhre Feinde abgebränt worden/ so bauwen sie andere/diesen gleich. Sihe/also prächtig vnd köstlich sind der
Indianer Palläst.

Wie sie

Wie der Floridaner Stätte erbauweisenen—Bry (1600)

Indiantown in Florida. The Seminoles mostly lived in *chickees*, which were structures approximately sixteen by nineteen feet, made mostly of parts of the palmetto tree. They were elevated about three feet off the ground, with a palmetto-thatched roof that was a work of art, smooth and compact inside, durable and watertight on the outside. Chickees were open on all sides to allow breezes to enter and were high enough off the ground to escape any floodwaters.

Map of the Peninsula of Florida—
Vinckeboons (1639?)
For being produced in the mid-seventeenth century, this Dutch map is remarkably accurate in its depiction of Cape Canaveral and the long barrier islands in the east, even showing palm trees near St. Augustine.

A

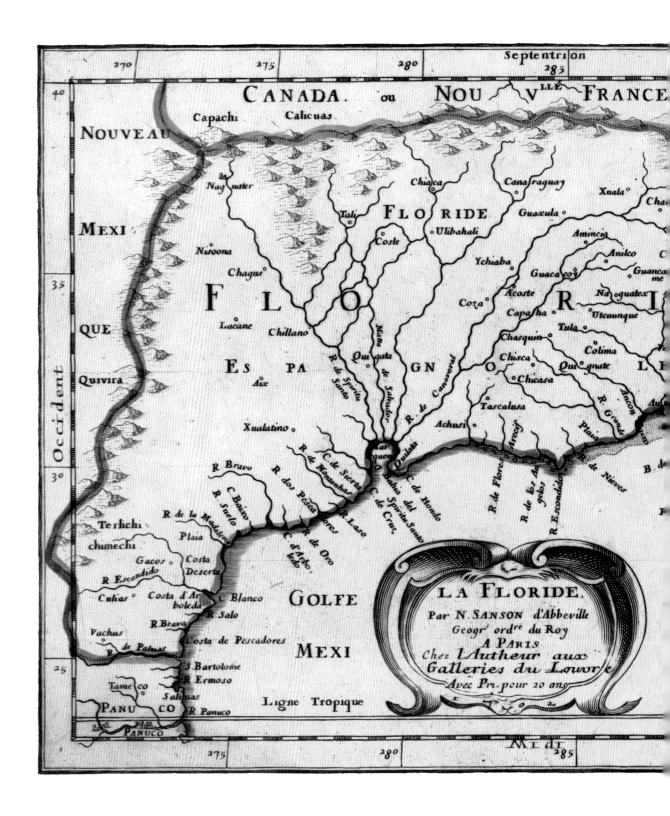

Septentrion

CANADA. ou NOUVᴸᴸᴱ FRANCE

270   275   280   285

40

NOUVEAU

Capachi   Calicuas

Nag~uater

MEXI

Chiaca   Canafraguay

Xuala

FLORIDE

Tali   Guaxula

Nisoona   Cosle   Ulibahali

Chagus   Amincia

35   Ychiaba   Anilco

FLO   Guaca co   Guanca me

Acoste   Na quatex

Coza   Capacha   Utcaunque

Lacane   Chillano   Chasquin   Tula   Colima

Es   Pa   GN   Chisca   Qui gnate

QUE   Chicasa

Quivira   Aix

R. de Spiritu Santo

Qui gata

Mata de Salvador

R. de Canaveral

Tascalusa   R. Grande

Xualatino   Achusi

Occident

R. de Sierra

Bahia del Spiritu Santo

C. de Hondo

R. de Flores   R. de los Angelos

R. Bravo   R. dos Pesca dores   R. Laso   C. de Cruz

30

C. Baico   R. de Oro

C. de Monanhan

R. Suelo   C. d'Arbo ledo

R. de la Madalena

Terlichi   Plaia

chimechi

Gacos   Costa Deserta

R. Escondido

Culias   Costa d'Ar boleda   C. Blanco

R. Salo   GOLFE

Vachus   R. Brava

R. de Palmas   Costa de Pescadores

25   S. Bartolome   MEXI

R. Ermoso

Tameco   Salinas

PANU CO   R. Panuco   Ligne Tropique

PANUCO

LA FLORIDE.
Par N. SANSON d'Abbeville
Geogrᵉ ordᵉ du Roy
A PARIS
Chez l'Autheur aux
Galleries du Louvre
Avec Priᵉ pour 20 ans

275   280   MIDI 285

La Floride; A Paris chez l'Auteur aux Galleries du Louvre. Avec Pri. pour 20 ans —Sanson d'Abbeville, Georgr. ordre. du Roÿ (1657)

This map depicts the coastline from Secotan in what used to be Virginia, but now is North Carolina, to the Planuco River in Mexico. French territory was to the north.

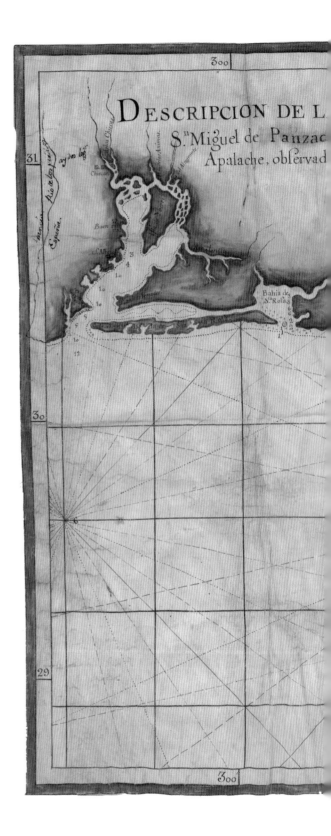

*Descripcion de la Bahia de Santa Maria de Galve,
y Puerto de Sn. Miguel de Panzacola con toda la costa
contigua y las demas bahias que tiene en ella, hasta
el Rio de Apalache; observada, y reconozida por los
ingenieros—Lajonk, y Siscara (1700)*

The French were looking for the source of all the rivers
that emptied into the Gulf of Mexico. After searching
the Apalachee area, they moved on to Pensacola Bay,
but saw the Spanish building a fort there and decided
to go to Mobile Bay.

HIA DE SANTA MARIA DE GALVE, Y PUERTO DE
toda la Costa contigua, y las demas Bahias que tiene en ella, hasta el Rio de
nozida por los Ingenieros Dn Jaime Lajonk, y Don Juan de Siscara.
1700

Tronco de dies, y siete leguas, castellanas, con que se mide este Mapa.

A Compleat Description of the Province of CAROLINA in 3 Parts. 1.The ... Mathews & Mr. John Love. 2. the West part by Cap. Tho. Nairn. 3. A Chart of the Coast ...

A MAP of SOUTH CAROLINA Shewing the Settlements of the ENGLISH FRENCH & INDIAN NATIONS from Charles Town to the River Missisipi by Capt. Tho. Nairn.

NORTH CAROLINA

SOUTH CAROLINA

PART OF NEW MEXICO

FRENCH SETLEMENT

FRENCH SETLEMENT

PART OF THE WESTERN OCEAN

PART OF THE BAY OF MEXICO

FLORIDA

Gulf of Florida

THE TOWN AND HARBOUR OF St AUGUSTIN

The Town The Castle

A Scale of Miles

COLLETON COUNTY

COLLETON COUNTY

GRANVILE COUNTY

ASHPO ISLAND

St HELENA SOUND

PORT ROYAL ISLAND ISLAND of St HELENA

at WAM BAHER

HUNTING ISLAND

PORT ROYAL

HILTONS HEAD ISLAND

PORT ROYAL SOUND

NEW LONDON

EDISTOW ISLAND

KATAWAH

To His Excellency WILLIAM LORD CRAVEN Palatine & the rest of the TRUE and ABSOLUTE LDS PROPRIETORS of the Province of CAROLINA This MAPP is Humbly Dedicated By EDW. CRISP

This Flourishing Province Produces Wine, Silk, Cotton, Indico, Rice, Pitch, Tar, Furrs, & other Valuable Commodytyes. Sold at the Carolina Coffee House in Birchin Lane London

Havana

C. Florida

GULF OF CUBA

THE GULF OF FLOR

Bahama Shoals

THE ISLAND OF BAHAMA

The Tropic of Cancer

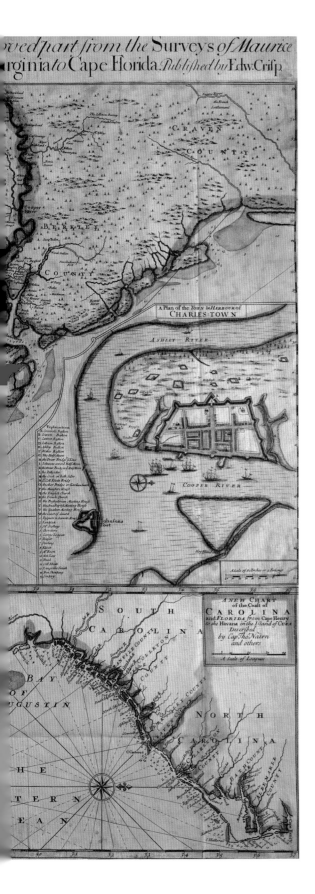

A compleat description of the province of Carolina in 3 parts: 1st, the improved part from the surveys of Maurice Mathews & Mr. John Love: 2ly, the west part by Capt. Tho. Nairn: 3ly, a chart of the coast from Virginia to Cape Florida—Harris (1711?)

With the establishment of Charles Town in the Carolina province in 1670, England challenged Spain's claim of exclusive rights to the entire East Coast. By 1700, a war in Europe between England, France, and Spain spread across the ocean, and Florida turned into a battlefield.

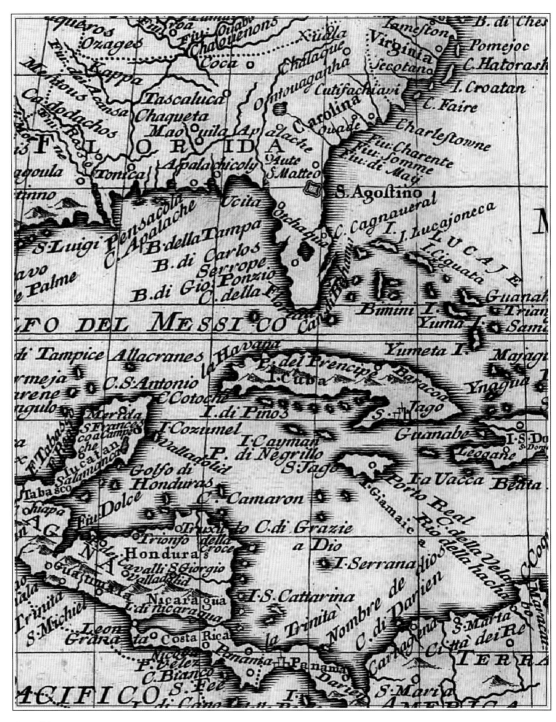

Detail from map on page 32

The Territorial Era and Antebellum Growth

DURING GRAND CEREMONIES AT ST. AUGUSTINE and Pensacola in 1821, Spanish flags were traded for U.S. flags as Andrew Jackson assumed his new role as Florida's first military governor. He made no secret of his dislike for the area, including the government home he deemed unfit to live in, but to his credit, the imperious governor did establish the necessary precedents for a new, non-Spanish government in three months before he returned to his Tennessee plantation.

Florida officially became the Territory of Florida in 1822, when the first territorial governor, William Duval, took over.

The Florida Legislative Council met in its first session that year at the western end of the territory in Pensacola, making it necessary for eastern delegates to travel a difficult fifty-nine days by ship. Those delegates were fortunate, though, because to reach the second session, western delegates were shipwrecked on their way east to St. Augustine, barely escaping with their lives. Not unexpectedly, the main topic of business during the second session was choosing a central location for the new capital. Tallahassee won, both for its locale and for its low incidence of yellow fever, a common problem in coastal areas. The third legislative session was held there in a primi-

tive two-story log cabin, but before long, a more substantial brick building took its place.

Inexpensive farmland lured cotton farmers, and soon, Florida had cotton plantations equal to those in nearby states. Impressive crops of sugar and indigo were also produced in Middle Florida, drawing more farmers there. The Seminoles, who didn't believe in land ownership, wanted fields to grow food for themselves and their families.

The military, too, moved into Florida, bringing along population and commerce. The Tampa Bay area benefited greatly when Fort Brooke was established. With the opening of a U.S. naval base in Key West, salvage work boomed due to the treacherous waters in the vicinity. An outbreak of yellow fever there in July 1823 took the lives of sixty-eight men, forcing the closure of the naval base for three months, but activity rebounded when it was reopened.

While Middle Florida was attracting farmers, people continued to move to the Gulf port of Apalachicola, a prime port for shipping cotton grown in more northern fields. To the west, despite much English, French, and Spanish competition, Pensacola continued to thrive. Though he never set foot there, Jacksonville was named for Andrew Jackson. Its location, on the St. Johns

River and on Florida's first significant road, drew residents, while St. Augustine long remained the city of importance on the east coast.

The ever-increasing expansion of farms, along with necessary land clearing, led to further clashes with the Seminoles, who needed land for their food production. Treaties were signed, only to be ignored later when white needs required it. The only solution, they believed, was to move the Seminoles off the lands.

When Andrew Jackson was elected president of the United States in 1828, he determined that the answer was to move all Indian tribes to Arkansas or Oklahoma, and accordingly, he signed the Indian Removal Act in 1830.

After several meetings between government agents and a group of chiefs, with much unproductive discussion, the discouraged chiefs sent scouts west to inspect the lands chosen for them. Displeased with what they saw, they returned, only to be tricked into signing a document they did not fully understand, in which they agreed to leave Florida.

Tensions continued to mount, and in 1835 two more unfortunate incidents took place. Near present-day Ocala, two officers were shot, killed, and scalped as they foolishly strolled outside Fort King. That same day, in what became known as the Dade Massacre, 110 men were ambushed as they began a march outside Fort Brooke, near Tampa. With that, the Second Seminole War began, the longest, most expensive Indian war in this nation's history.

During this war, Osceola, a Seminole hero, was captured in a shameful episode when the U.S. military sent him a message saying it wished to hold peace talks and he agreed. Carrying a flag of truce, Osceola and his party arrived at the meeting. They were engaged in preliminary small talk when he suddenly realized that armed soldiers surrounded him and his group. He knew he had been deceived.

Shortly, he and his group were imprisoned. Most Americans were appalled at this incidence of white man's treachery. Osceola died of a severely infected sore throat in January 1838 after a few months in a South Carolina prison, a sad postscript to a tragic chapter in our national history.

The war was probably one of the most frustrating, since eight U.S. commanding officers took turns trying to win it and each gave up and left. Discouragement grew, too, among the outnumbered Seminoles, who were disheartened over the loss of lives, the loss of land, the broken treaties. Then, too, large numbers of slaves who had joined with the Seminoles must have known the dire fate that awaited them if captured. Seeing no way out, many Seminoles and slaves started the trek west.

President John Tyler ended the Second Seminole War in 1842, but the Florida territory went into a temporary slump. As prospects gradually began to improve, the idea of statehood entered conversations more and more.

An application for statehood was made at a time when tensions were high in Congress over maintaining a balance in the young country between free states and slave states. Fortunately for Florida, the free state of Iowa was applying to join the United States at the same time as Florida. Both were accepted, and in 1845, Florida became the twenty-seventh state.

With statehood came a recovery from the dismal days following the war. The ports of

Tampa and Jacksonville experienced an increase in commerce. Cotton and sugar production surged in Middle Florida, while newly planted tobacco became highly profitable.

The cattle industry, made up of the descendents of the wild cattle escapees from early Spanish explorers, was born in Florida, not in the Wild West as Hollywood would have us believe. Cowmen shipped their cattle from ports in the Sunshine State to New York and Cuba.

Conflicts with the Indians, however, continued as the Black Seminoles were a particularly vexing factor. Many runaway slaves had joined the Seminoles, were accepted by them, and were considered by them to be mostly free. Americans did not agree, which kept trouble simmering until 1855 when whites confiscated some crops belonging to a Seminole chief, Billy Bowlegs, and destroyed the rest. The enraged chief insisted he be paid for his valuable crops, but he was snubbed, causing the Third Seminole War to start. It lasted until 1858, but unlike the first two wars, it consisted mostly of sporadic and unenthusiastic skirmishes.

Considering their familiarity with abundant wild game, rivers full of fish, and plant foods that grew wild, the Seminole, unlike the whites, could not be starved into defeat. Both sides were weary, but after first refusing to move west, Billy Bowlegs eventually accepted the cash offer from the whites and his tribe made a dismal journey to Indian Territory. About two hundred Seminoles did not. They fled into the Everglades swamp, secure in the knowledge that whites would not follow.

As the states of the North and South moved ever further apart on the issue of slavery, many Floridians sided with their Southern neighbors on that point and on the possibility of secession.

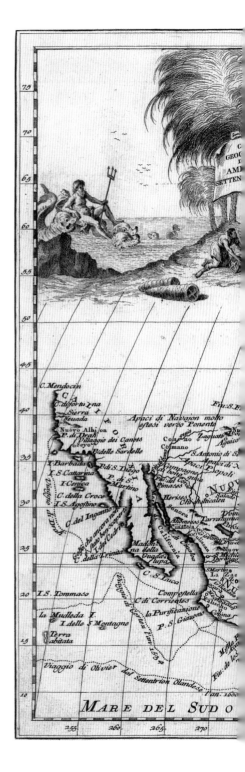

Carta geografica dell' America settentrionale—L'Isle (1750)
This map was produced by Guillaume de L'Isle, a Parisian who became the most famous mapmaker of his time. The influence of his training in astronomy and mathematics is apparent when this map is compared with maps by others who preferred to emphasize their artistic qualities.

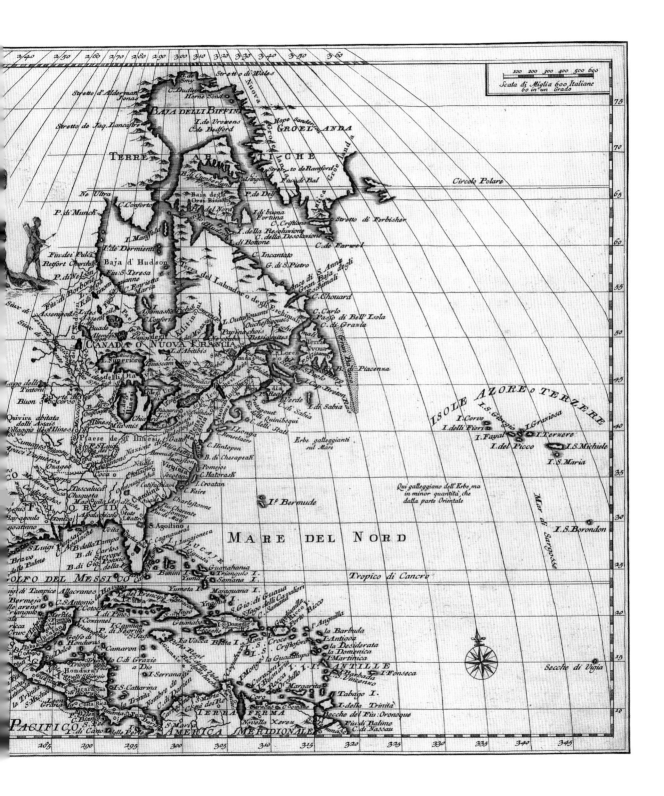

Scala di Miglia 600 Italiane
60 in un Grado

Stretto di Wales
Stretto d'Alderman Jonas
BAIA DELLI BIFFINI
Stretto de Jaq Lancastre
GROELANDA
TERRE ARTICHE
Circolo Polare

Ne Ultra
P. di Munch
C. Conforto
Stretto di Forbisher
I. di buona Fortuna
C. Cristiano
I. della Resolutione
C. della Desolatione
di Bottone
C. de Farwel

Fiu dei Pulci
Retfort Churchill
Baja d'Hudson
C. Incantato
G. di S. Pietro

P. di Borbone
P. di Nelson
Fiu S. Teresa
Anse di S. Anna
Gran Baja degli
Eschimali
C. Chouard

CANADA o NUOVA FRANCIA
C. Carlo
Passo di Bell' Isola
C. di Grazia

Lago Superiore
B. di Piacenza
ISOLE AZORE o TERZERE
I. Corvo
I. delli Fiori
I.S. Giorgio
I. Graziosa
I. Fayal
I. Terzero
I. del Picco
I.S. Michiele
I.S. Maria

Quivira abitata
dalli Assais
Villaggio degl'Illines
Paese di S. Illinesi
Erbe galleggianti
sul Mare

Xumattes
Apaci Vaqueros
Ozages
C. Hinlopen
B. di Chesapeak
Pomcioe
C. Hatorask
I. Croatan
C. Faire
Virginia

I. Bermude

Qui galleggiano dell'Erbe, ma
in minor quantità, che
dalla parte Orientale

Tuscaluca
Chaqueta
FIORIDA
Mar di Sargosse
I.S. Borondon

S. Agostino

MARE DEL NORD

S. Luigi
B. della Tampa
B. di Carlos
Bravo
B. di Palme
Guanahania

Tropico di Cancro

GOLFO DEL MESSICO
Bimini I.
Triangulo I.
Samana I.

Alfi di Tampice Alacranes
C.S. Antonio
Yumeta I.
Maraguana I.
Secche di Vigia

I. del Principe
I. di Pinos
S. Jago
Gvanabo
I. Domenico
Porto Ricco
l'Anguilla
la Barbuda
l'Antigoa
la Desiderata
la Domenica
Martinica
ANTILLE
I. Fonseca

Golfo di Honduras
Camaron
C. di Grazie
a Dio
I. Serrana
la Guadalupa

Honduras
I.S. Cattarina

Nombre de
Dios
TERRA FERMA
Tabago I.
I. della Trinità
Bocche del Fiu Oronoque

PACIFICO
AMERICA MERIDIONALE
Novella Xarex
Fiu di Balme
C. di Nassau

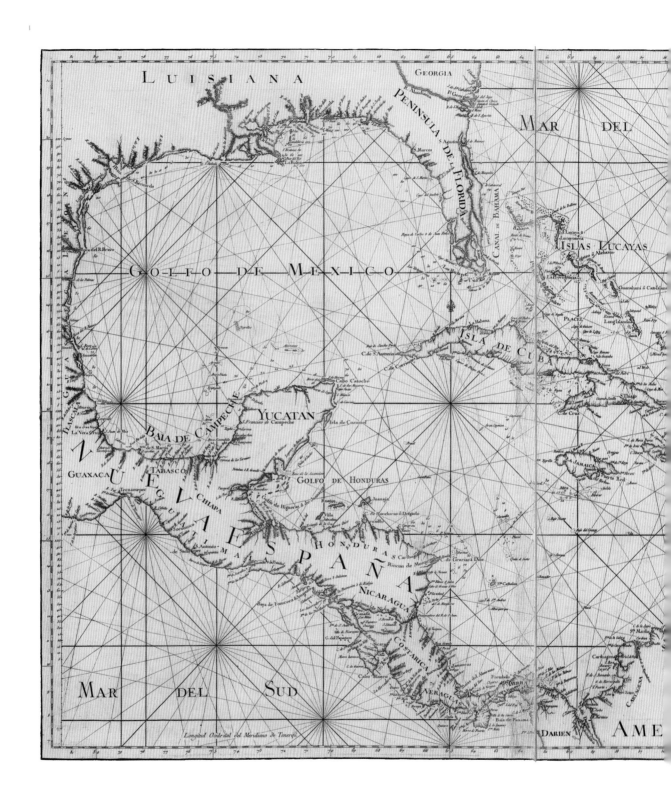

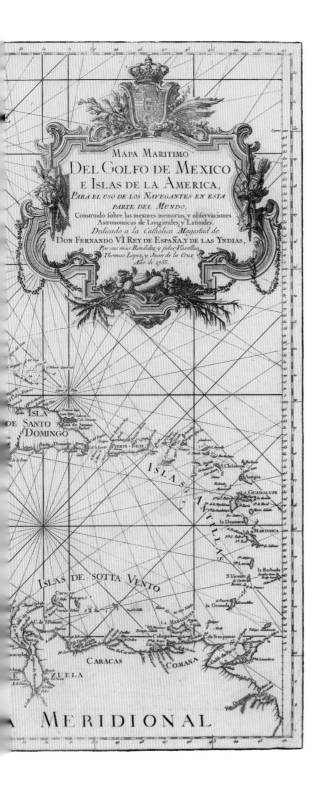

*Mapa maritimo del Golfo de Mexico e islas de la America,
para el uso de los navegantes en esta parte del mundo,
construido sobre las mexores memorias, y observaciones
astronomicas de longitudes, y latitudes. Dedicado a la
Catholica Magestad de Don Fernando VI Rey de España,
y de las Yndias, por sus mas rendidos, y fieles vasallos—
Lopez, y La Cruz (1755)*

This is a meticulously drawn map for the use of navigators,
showing the Gulf of Mexico and the islands of the Caribbean.
It also emphasizes why Florida has the sense of being more
Caribbean as Cuba is just ninety miles away and the Bahama
Islands are even closer to her eastern shore.

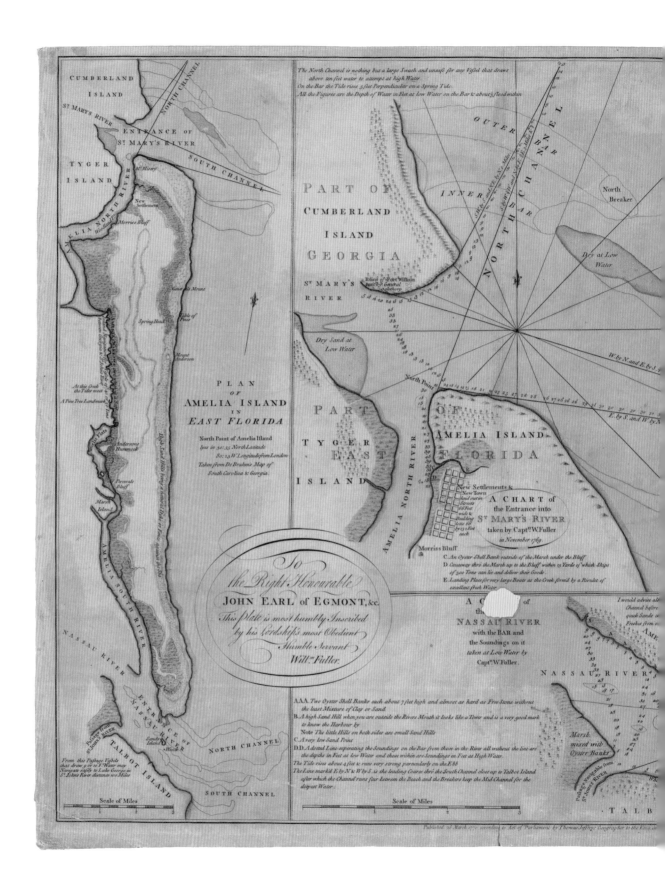

CUMBERLAND ISLAND

ST MARYS RIVER

TYGER ISLAND

AMELIA NORTH RIVER

NORTH CHANNEL

ENTRANCE OF ST MARY'S RIVER

SOUTH CHANNEL

Mt Misery

New Settlement
Woodland
Morries Bluff

Sea Gulls Mount

Spring Head
Table of Pines

Mount Anderson

At this Creek the Tide meet
A Pine Tree Landmark

High Land 1000 Yards a natural Dyke at Face against the Sea

Sunds Flats
Andersons Hummock

Peracals Bluff

March Island

AMELIA SOUTH RIVER

NASSAU RIVER

The North Channel is nothing but a large Swash and unsafe for any Vessel that draws above ten feet water to attempt at high Water.
On the Bar the Tide rises 5 feet Perpendicular on a Spring Tide.
All the Figures are the Depth of Water in Feet at Low Water on the Bar & about ⅓ flood within

OUTER BAR

INNER BAR

NORTH CHANNEL

North Breaker

Dry at Low Water

PART OF CUMBERLAND ISLAND GEORGIA

ST MARY'S RIVER

Ruins of Fort William built by General Oglethorp

Dry Sand at Low Water

PART OF TYGER EAST ISLAND

North Point

AMELIA NORTH RIVER

OF AMELIA ISLAND FLORIDA

New Settlements & New Town laid out in Streets 66 Feet wide & Building lots 60 by 132 Feet each

Morriss Bluff

W by N and E by S

E by S and W by N

PLAN OF AMELIA ISLAND IN EAST FLORIDA

North Point of Amelia Island
lies in 30:55 North Latitude
80:23 W Longitude from London
Taken from De Brahms Map of
South Carolina & Georgia

A CHART of the Entrance into ST MARY'S RIVER taken by Captn Wm Fuller in November 1769

C. An Oyster Shell Bank outside of the Marsh under the Bluff.
D. Causeway thro' the Marsh up to the Bluff within 15 Yards of which Ships of 300 Tons can lie and deliver their Goods.
E. Landing Place for very large Boats at the Creek formd by a Rivulet of excellent fresh Water.

To the Right Honourable JOHN EARL of EGMONT, &c. This Plate is most humbly Inscribed by his Lordship's most Obedient Humble Servant Willm Fuller.

NASSAU RIVER

ENTRANCE OF NASSAU RIVER

Sandy Island
Wreck

NORTH CHANNEL

TALBOT ISLAND

SOUTH CHANNEL

From this Passage Vessels that draw 9 or 10 f Water may Navigate safely to Lake George in St Johns River distance 100 Miles

A CHART of the NASSAU RIVER with the BAR and the Soundings on it taken at Low Water by Captn Wm Fuller.

NASSAU RIVER

Marsh mixed with Oyster Banks

passage navigable from St Marys River

I would advise all
Channel before
quick Sands
Freshes from

AAA. Two Oyster Shell Banks each about 7 feet high and almost as hard as Free Stone without the least Mixture of Clay or Sand.
B. A high Sand Hill when you are outside the Rivers Mouth it looks like a Tower and is a very good mark to know the Harbour by
Note The little Hills on both sides are small Sand Hills
C. A very low Sand Point
DD. A dotted Line separating the Soundings on the Bar from those in the River all without the line are the depths in Feet at low Water and those within are Soundings in Feet at High Water
The Tide rises about 4 feet & runs very strong particularly on the Ebb
The Line markd E by N & W by S is the leading Course thro' the South Channel close up to Talbot Island after which the Channel runs far between the Beach and the Breakers keep the Mid Channel for the deepest Water

Scale of Miles

Scale of Miles

Published 18 March 1770 according to Act of Parliament by Thomas Jefferys Geographer to the King

TALB

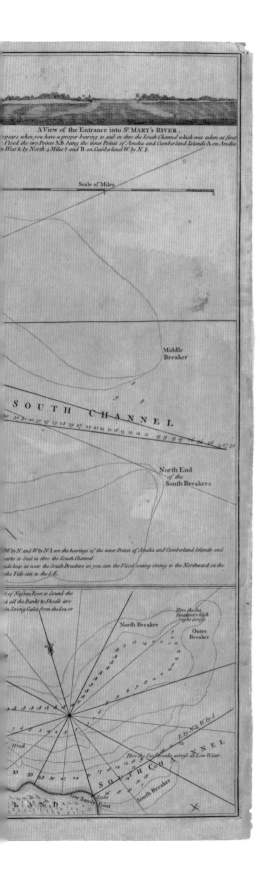

A View of the Entrance into St. MARY's RIVER.

appears when you have a proper bearing to sail in thro the South Channel which was taken at first Flood the two Points A.B. being the inner Points of Amelia and Cumberland Islands A on Amelia n West & by North 4 Miles ½ and B. on Cumberland W. by N. ½.

Scale of Miles

Middle Breaker

SOUTH CHANNEL

North End of the South Breakers

W by N. and W by N ½ are the bearings of the inner Points of Amelia and Cumberland Islands and marks to Sail in thro the South Channel do keep as near the South Breakers as you can the Flood setting strong to the Northward on the the Tide sett to the S.E.

of Nassau River to Sound the all the Banks & Shoals are in Strong Gales from the Sea or

North Breaker

Outer Breaker

Here the Sea breakers high right across

Here the Sea breaks across at Low Water

Wreck

E.N. N & W. by S

SOUTH CHANNEL

LAND

long Sandy Point

Stake

South Breaker

Plan of Amelia Island in East Florida, north point of Amelia Island lyes in 30:55 north latitude 80:23 w. longitude from London, taken from De Brahm's Map of South Caroline & Georgia. A chart of the entrance into St. Mary's River, taken by W. Fuller in November 1769. A c[hart] of the [mouth of] Nassau River with the bar and the soundings on it, taken at low water by W. Fuller. To the Right Honourable John Earl of Egmont &c. this plate is most humbly inscribed by his lordship's most obedient humble servant— Fuller (1770)

Amelia Island, at the southernmost tip of a chain of barrier islands that stretch from South Carolina to Florida, was the most northern Florida settlement. When Spain allied with England against France, and the United States prepared for the War of 1812 against England, Amelia Island was an important neutral port for U.S. merchants.

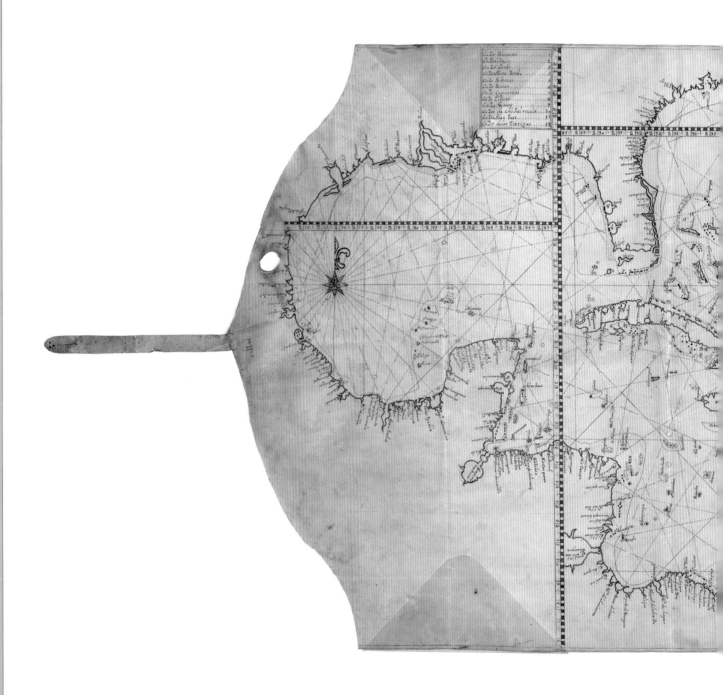

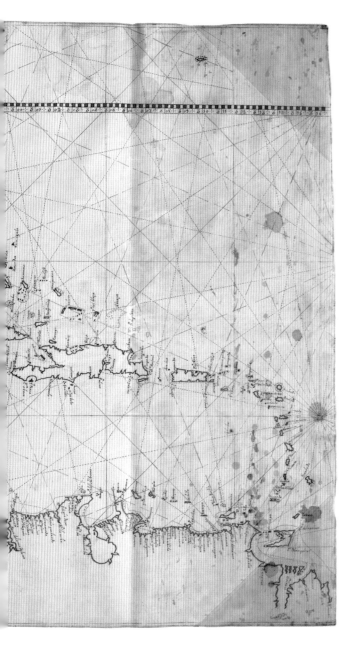

Map showing Caribbean area including
West Indies and Gulf of Mexico—
unknown (ca. 1770)
This map was almost certainly intended for maritime use as it was drawn on vellum, a type of animal skin treated to render it waterproof, important on sea-going vessels. The map could be rolled up and secured with the narrow extension visible on the left.

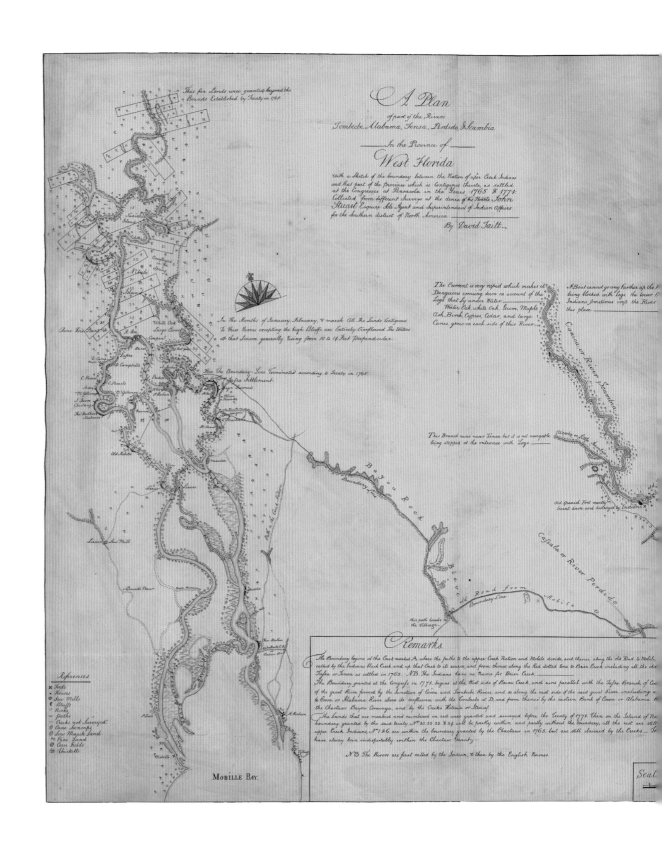

A Plan
of part of the Rivers
Tombecbe, Alabama, Tensa, Perdido, & Scambia

In the Province of

West Florida

with a Sketch of the boundary between the Nation of upper Creek Indians
and that part of the province which is Contiguous thereto, as settled
at the Congresses at Pensacola in the Years 1765 & 1771.
Collected from different Surveys at the desire of the Hon'ble John
Stuart Esquire Sole Agent and Superintendant of Indian Affairs
for the Southern district of North America.

By David Taitt

These few Lands were granted beyond the Bounds Established by Treaty in 1765.

In the Months of January, February, & March All the Lands Contiguous to these Rivers excepting the high Bluffs are Entirely Overflowed The Waters at that Season generally rising from 10 to 14 Feet Perpendicular.

The Current is very rapid which makes it Dangerous coming down on account of the Logs that lye under Water.
Water Oak, white Oak, Gum, Maple Ash, Birch, Cypress, Cedar, and large Canes grow on each side of this River.

A Boat cannot go any further up the being blocked with Logs. the lower Indians sometimes cross the River this place

Here The Boundary-Line Terminated according to Treaty in 1765.

This Branch runs near Tensa but it is not navigable being stopped at the entrance with Logs.

MOBILLE BAY.

References
x Forts
. Houses
Saw Mills
Bluffs
Rocks
— paths
Creeks not Surveyed
Cane Swamps
Low Marsh Land
Pine Land
Corn fields
Thickets

Remarks.

The Boundary begins at the Creek marked A, where the paths to the upper Creek Nation and Mobile divide, and thence along the old Road to Mobile, called by the Indians black Creek, and up that Creek to its source, and from thence along the Red dotted line to Brier Creek including all the old Tesfra or Tensa as settled in 1765. N.B. The Indians have no Name for Brier Creek.

The Boundary granted at the Congress in 1771 begins at the West side of Brier Creek, and runs parallel with the Tesfra Branch of the great River formed by the Junction of Cusa and Tombecbe Rivers, and so along the east side of the said great River including to Cusa or Alabama River above its confluence with the Tombecbe at D, and from thence by the eastern Bank of Cusa or Alabama the Chactaws Bayou Conunga, and by the Creeks Hitcisa or Stencos.

The Lands that are marked and numbered in red were granted and surveyed before the Treaty of 1771. Then on the Island of Ne boundary granted by the said treaty, N° 30. 53. 33. & 34 will be partly within and partly without the boundary, all the rest are settl upper Creek Indians, N° 1 & 6 are within the boundary granted by the Chactaws in 1765, but are still claimed by the Creeks. have always been indisputably within the Chactaw Grant.

N.B The Rivers are first called by the Indians, & then by the English Names.

Scal

40

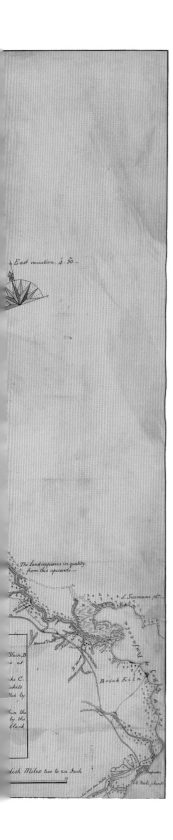

*A plan of part of the rivers Tombecbe, Alabama, Tensa, Perdido, & Scambia
in the province of West Florida; with a sketch of the boundary between the nation
of upper Creek Indians and that part of the province which is contigious* [sic]
*thereto, as settled at the congresses at Pensacola in the years 1765 & 1771.
Collected from different surveys at the desire of the Hon' ble John Stuart, Esquire,
sole agent and superintendant of Indian Affairs for the southern district of North
America—Taitt (1771?)*

David Taitt, originally from Scotland, worked as a surveyor for the British government.
He became known as an excellent mapmaker, producing outstanding work notable for
its precision and accuracy. This map is still highly regarded.

*Thomas Hutchins' land grant and map to 2000 acres
in West Florida—Durnford (1776)*

Thomas Hutchins, a military engineer, cartographer, geographer, and surveyor, was the first and last to hold the title "Geographer of the United States."
The title was changed to "Surveyor General" for his successor. Hutchins
was an early proponent of Manifest Destiny. This map shows a land grant
awarded to him, four miles east of the Mississippi River.

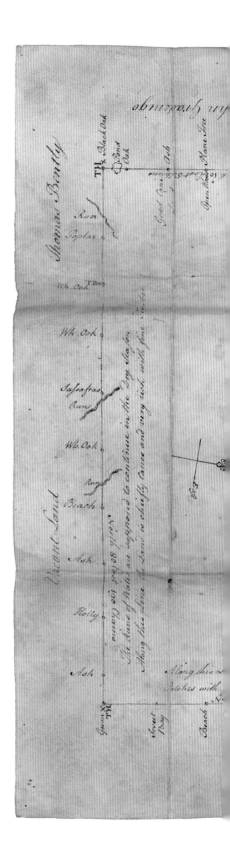

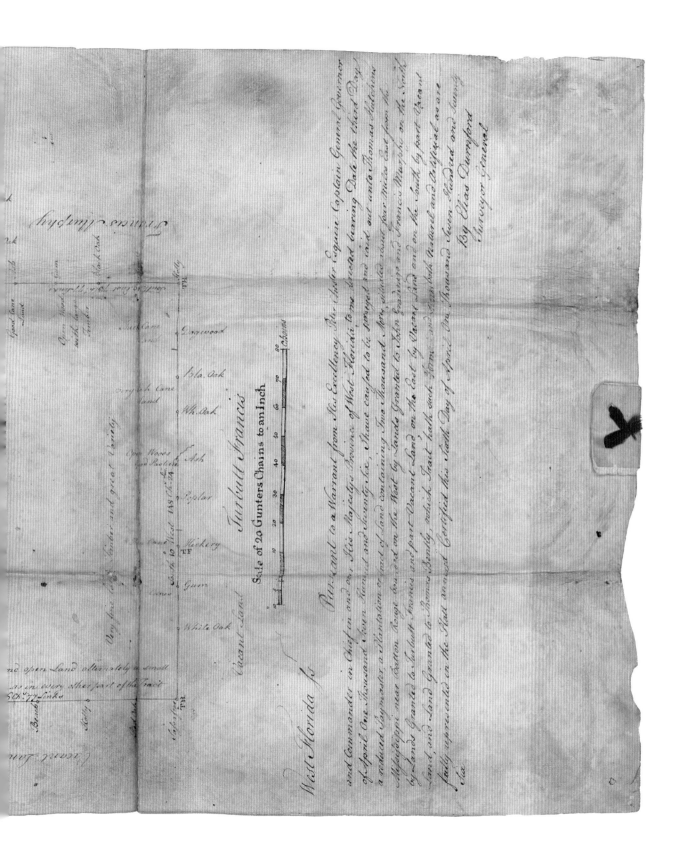

Francis Murphy

Turbutt Francis

Scale of 20 Gunters Chains to an Inch

Vacant Land

West Florida ƒs

Holly
Dogwood
Bla. Oak
Wh. Oak
Ash
Poplar
Hickery
Gum
White Oak

Pursuant to a Warrant from His Excellency Peter Chester Esquire Captain General Governor and Commander in Chief in and over His Majestys Province of West Florida &c. bearing Date the third Day of April One Thousand Seven hundred and Seventy Six, I have caused to be surveyed and laid out unto Thomas Hutchins a reduced Paymaster a Plantation or tract of Land containing Two thousand acres pleasant about four miles East from the Mississippi near Cotton Bend bounded on the West by Lands Granted to John Gaillarge and Francis Murphe on the North by Land Granted to Turbutt Francis and part Vacant Land on the East by Vacant Land and on the South by part Vacant Land and Land Granted to Thomas Bartley, which Tract hath such Form and Marks both Antient and artificial as are fully represented on the Plat annexed Certified this sixth Day of April One thousand Seven hundred and twenty Six

By Elias Durnford
Surveyor General

A general map of the southern British colonies in America, comprehending North and South Carolina, Georgia, East and West Florida, with the neighboring Indian countries, from the modern surveys of Engineer de Brahm, Capt. Collet, Mouzon, & others, and from the large hydrographical survey of the coasts of East and West Florida—Romans (1776)

This map was produced by Bernard Romans, a Dutch-born American navigator, cartographer, soldier, engineer, and writer, who traveled widely in Florida by boat and on foot. He published *A Concise Natural History of East and West Florida,* an eight-hundred-page book with highly respected maps and charts.

PLAN OF CHARLESTOWN.

References
a. State House
b. Church
A. Watch House
e. S.t Phillips Church
E. Exchange
g. Work House

PLAN OF S.t AUGUSTINE.

References
a. Fort S.t Mark
b. Governors House
c. Parade
d. a Church
e. Guard House
f. Parish Church
g. Franciscan Fryars
h. Dutch Church

A GENERAL MAP OF THE
SOUTHERN BRITISH COLONIES,
IN AMERICA.
comprehending
NORTH AND SOUTH CAROLINA,
GEORGIA,
EAST AND WEST FLORIDA.
with THE NEIGHBOURING INDIAN COUNTRIES,
From the Modern Surveys of
Engineer de Brahm, Capt. Collet, Mouzon & Others;
and from the Large Hydrographical Survey of the Coasts
of East and West Florida.
BY B. ROMANS,
1776.

London, Printed for R.Sayer and J.Bennett, Map, Chart and Printsellers, N.o 53 Fleet Street, as the Act directs, 15.t Oct.r 1776.

Scale of 220 Fathoms or ¼ of a Mile, (60¼ to a Degree)

¼ Mile

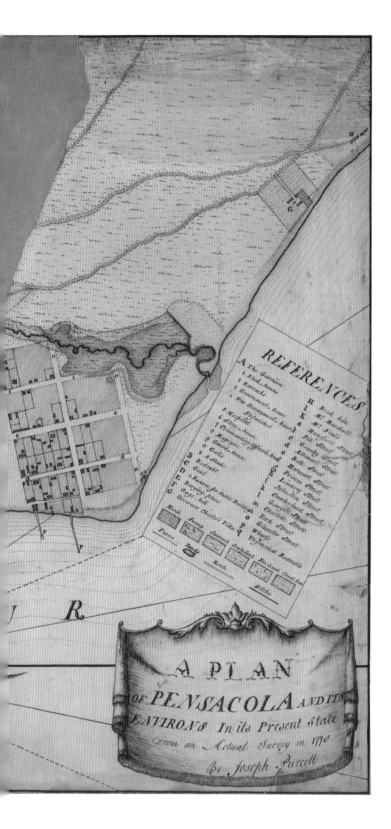

A plan of Pensacola and its environs in its present state, from an actual survey—Purcell (1778)

Pensacola functioned as the capital of West Florida while under British control from 1763 to 1781. The English made a lasting contribution to the city with its plan and street grid, pictured here and mostly all still in use.

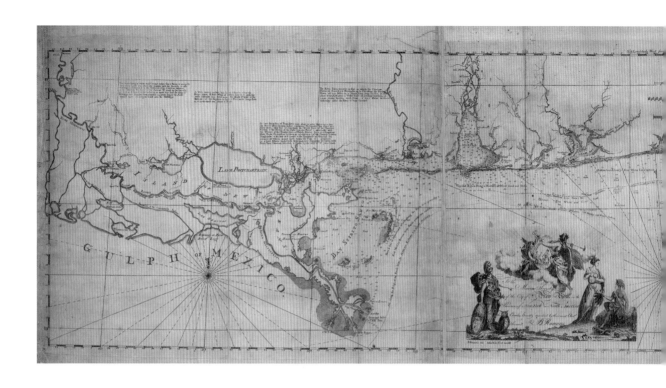

Maps of East and West Florida—Romans (1781)

Here are two other maps from Bernard Romans, published in 1781, six years after his famous book, *A Concise History of East and West Florida.* The larger map contains a view of St. Marys River, which forms part of the border between Georgia and Florida and is the most southern point of Georgia. Actual size of the larger map is about ninety-three inches long.

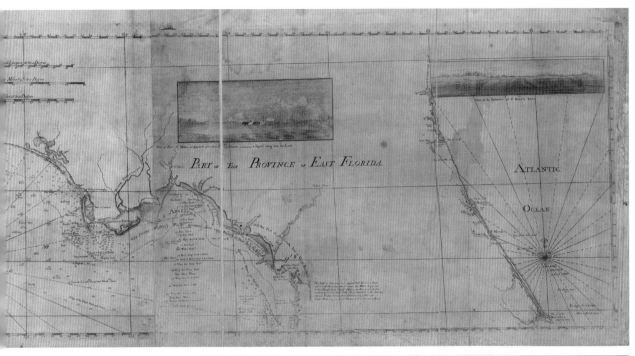

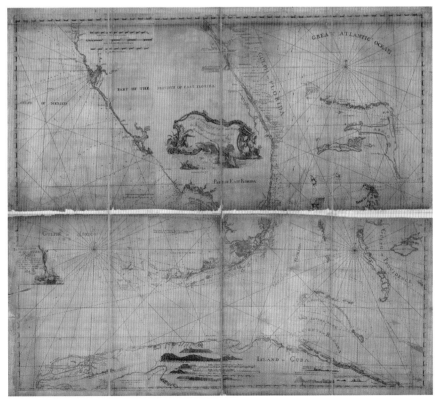

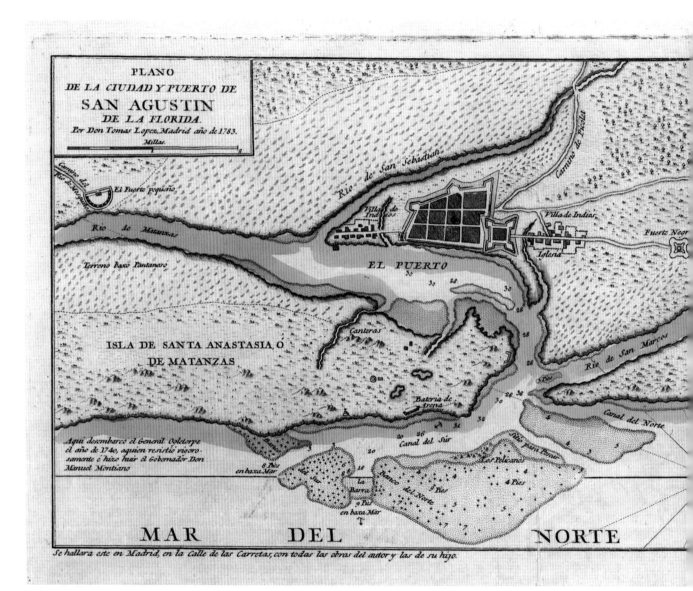

PLANO
DE LA CIUDAD Y PUERTO DE
SAN AGUSTIN
DE LA FLORIDA.
Por Don Tomas Lopez, Madrid año de 1783.
Millas.

EL PUERTO

ISLA DE SANTA ANASTASIA, Ó
DE MATANZAS

Aqui desembarco el General Ogletorpe
el año de 1740, aquien resistio vigoro-
samente é hizo huir el Gobernador Don
Manuel Montiano

MAR   DEL   NORTE

Se hallara este en Madrid, en la Calle de las Carretas, con todas las obras del autor y las de su hijo.

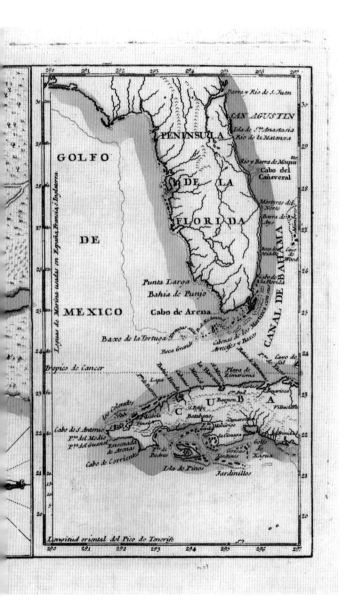

*Plano de la ciudad y puerto de San Agustin
de la Florida—López de Vargas Machuca (1783)*
A map of America's first port city, St. Augustine, shows the shallowness of the waters in the harbor, which prevented the entry of large vessels. While it could be a disadvantage, the inconvenience surely contributed to the preservation of St. Augustine's charm. The Matanzas River might be the world's only river named for a massacre, the slaughtering of French Huguenots by Spanish forces in 1565.

Bahia de Tampa—Dericción de Hidrografia (1809)

Tampa Bay, the largest open water estuary in Florida, was visited by Ponce de León in 1521, then by Hernando de Soto in 1539, and then mostly ignored for two hundred years. It was and remains a shelter for two hundred species of fish and a year-round home to twenty-five species of birds. Warm water around the bay has drawn manatees, shrimp, and crabs and supplied nesting sites for herons, brown pelicans, egrets, and cormorants from earliest times.

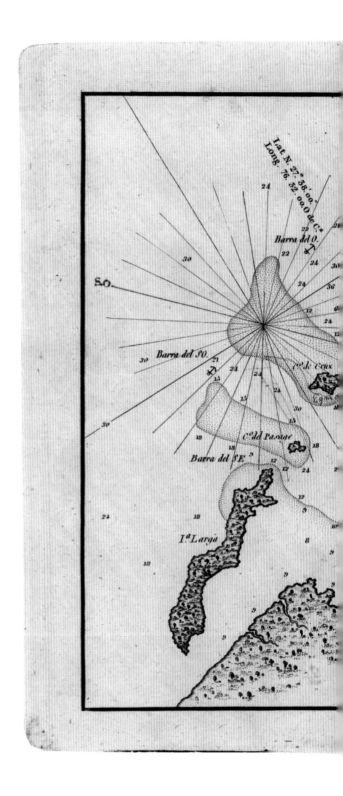

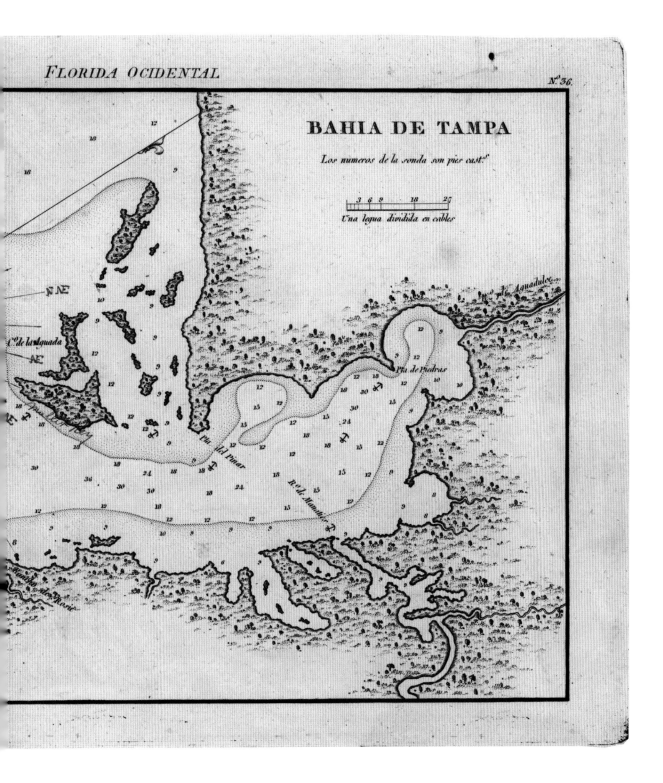

BAHIA DE TAMPA

Los numeros de la sonda son pies cast.

Una legua dividida en cables

Map of the lands belonging to R. S. Hackley,
esq., in east Florida—Hackley (1823?)
President James Monroe appointed R. S. Hackley, Esq., to be Inspector
of Revenue at St. Augustine when Spain ceded Florida to the United
States. None of Monroe's appointments met with the approval of Gen.
Andrew Jackson, including this one.

No. 30.
CHECK ANSWERS.
FLORIDA.

1. *Situation.*—Between 24° 30′ and 31° north latitude, and 3° 16′ and 10° 13′ west longitude.
2. *Boundaries.*—On the north, Georgia and Alabama; south, Gulf of Florida; east, Atlantic Ocean; west, Gulf of Mexico and Perdido River.
3. *Principal towns.*—St. Augustine, Pensacola, St. Mark's, Poppa.
4. *Rivers.*—St. John's, Appalachicola, Perdido, Charlotte.
5. *Population* in 1820—estimated at 10,000.
6. *Area*—57,750 square miles.

Geographical conversation cards: states of the United States— Melish (1824)

John Melish, originally from Scotland, was a Philadelphia map publisher who, in 1816, issued the first wall map showing the United States with British and Spanish possessions. It proved to be so popular that twenty-three editions followed. Each playing card in this set represented one state or U.S. territory, with question and answer cards included.

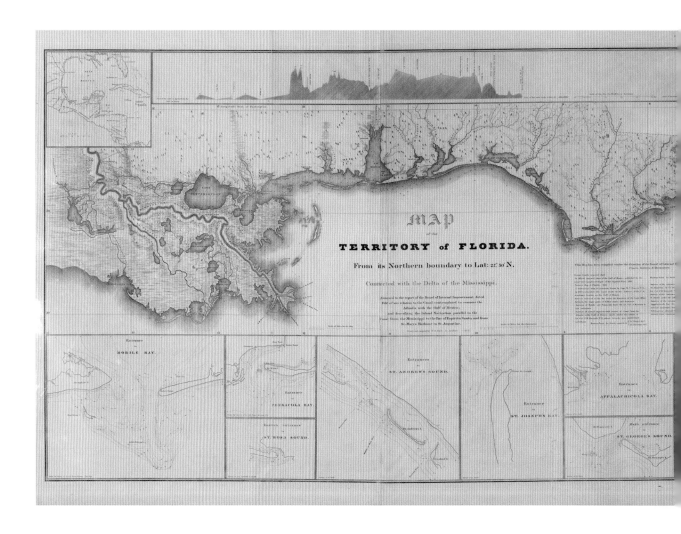

MAP
of the
TERRITORY of FLORIDA.

From its Northern boundary to Lat: 27° 30' N.

Connected with the Delta of the Mississippi.

Map of the territory of Florida, from its northern boundary to lat. 27°30'N, connected with the delta of the Mississippi: annexed to the report of the Board of Internal Improvement dated Febr. 19th, 1829, relating to the canal contemplated to connect the Atlantic with the Gulf of Mexico and describing the inland navigation parallel to the coast from the Mississippi to the Bay of Espiritu Santo and from St. Mary's Harbour to St. Augustine. This map has been compiled under the direction of the Board of Internal Improvement—Swift (1829)

As far back as 1567, the idea of carving a canal across the Florida peninsula attracted supporters. Survey parties toured projected routes and submitted a report in 1829, but money, as always, was a problem. The project was periodically proposed over the years, most recently in the 1960s.

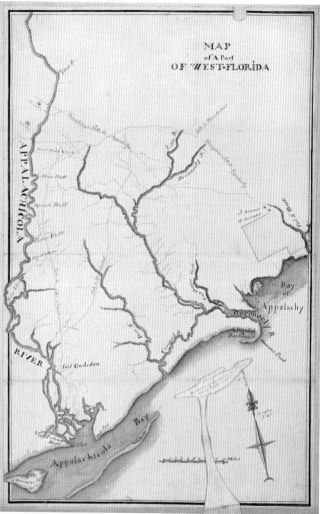

Map of a part of west-Florida—unknown (18--)
The Apalachicola River formed the boundary between East Florida and West Florida, and except for the area around its mouth, the river is now the boundary between the Eastern and the Central time zones. The Apalachicola Bay is a lagoon, long famous for its oysters.

Seat of War—U.S. Army Corps of Engineers (1839)

This map shows the Seat of War in Florida in 1835, with the military road from Fort Brooke on Tampa Bay to Fort King, located near modern-day Ocala. The map also shows the battleground where, in 1835, the Seminoles killed Major Dade and his men in what became known as the Dade Massacre.

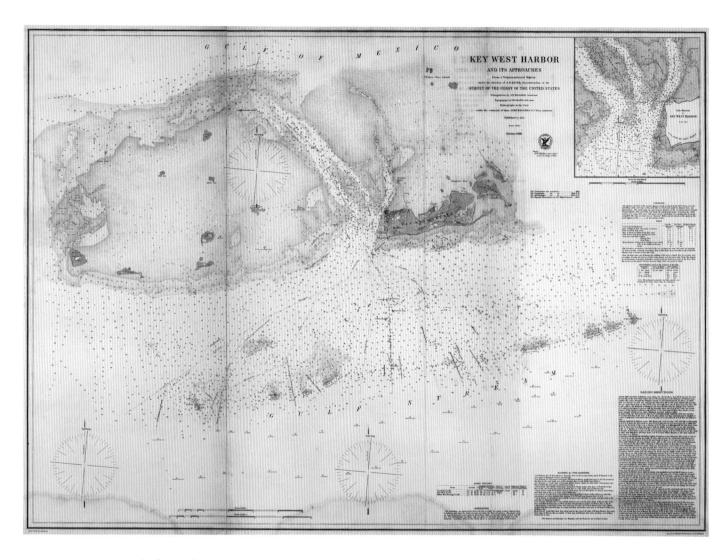

Key West harbor and its approaches—From a trigonometrical survey under the direction of A. D. Bache, Superintendent of the survey of the coast of the United States. Triangulation by J. E. Hilgard, Assistant. Topography by L. H. Adams, Sub-Asst. Hydrography by the party under the command of Lieut. John Rodgers, U.S. Navy Assistant. Redd. drng. by E. K. Knorr. Engd. by E. Yeager, E. F. Woodward, and H. M. Knight (1855)

Fort Taylor was built in 1845 to protect Key West harbor. Federal forces held the fort during the Civil War. Key West played a major role in the war because of its strategic location. The Union blockading forces were stationed there during the entire war.

The Civil War

ABRAHAM LINCOLN'S NAME WAS NOT ON FLORIDA ballots for the presidential election of 1860. When news of his win reached the state, the *Tallahassee Floridian and Journal* ominously proclaimed: "Lincoln is elected. There is a beginning of the end."

Following the lead of South Carolina and Mississippi secessionists, Florida seceded from the Union in January 1861, just fifteen years after joining it. With this action, bitterness between Unionists and secessionists in the state intensified. Most Southerners believed that Lincoln was a threat to their way of life and that war was inevitable, but would be brief, which probably contributed to a swelling in the numbers of volunteers to the army. By February, Florida joined six other Southern states to form the Confederate States of America. Two months later, when the Union commander of Fort Sumter at Charleston, South Carolina, refused to surrender the fort to the provisional Confederate commander, the Confederates opened fire and the Civil War had begun.

Union forces quickly seized control of Fort Taylor at Key West and Fort Jefferson on the Dry Tortugas. A few months later, they reinforced control of Fort Pickens at Pensacola Bay and made it their Florida headquarters for the duration of the war. Soon after, Apalachicola was nearly completely vacated, Fernandina and St. Augustine were federally occupied, and Jacksonville began enduring the first of four occupations, worsened by deliberately set fires.

Because of her sparse population and minimal industries, the state of Florida played a relatively small part in the Civil War; the majority of her troops were sent to participate in major battles beyond her borders. The units left behind managed to repel some lesser raids along the coast and were involved in Jacksonville's periodic takeovers.

Most of the Florida coastline was under Union command, enabling them to frequently disrupt shipments of food, supplies, and munitions to Southern forces. The Confederates considered control of the center of the state crucial in order to protect food produced on farms, cattle from ranches, and salt, needed to preserve meat and to tan leather goods. Workers along the Panhandle coastline turned out salt by boiling seawater or by evaporating it in artificial pools.

In April 1862 the Confederate States authorized the first national military conscription in

American history, drafting all men ages eighteen to thirty-five, then shortly increasing it to those between seventeen and forty-five. The new law had enormous effect on the meagerly populated state, and on women in particular. The exit of able-bodied men made it necessary for the women left behind to do men's jobs. They worked the farms, planting, harvesting, doing blacksmith work, butchering, driving oxcarts to haul cotton and other crops, and overseeing slave laborers, all the while maintaining their homes and caring for their children.

Any food, clothing, medicines, or other supplies they could not produce for their families were usually hard or impossible to buy. Coffee at $100 a pound was an unaffordable luxury for years. Women used substitutes—toasted grains for coffee, cornmeal for wheat flour, starch made from coontie, an old Seminole method. Since they had no spare time, they knitted and sewed clothing for their families and the troops while they prayed.

The physical demands on women were more than matched by the mental stress of being the protectors of their families. The anxiety of overseeing slaves at work and the possibility of handling an uprising should one begin were paramount in the minds of many women.

Probably nothing impacted Florida's history more than the enslavement of black people, the effects of which touched every aspect of every life. Though slaves had some pleasures in their lives, these pleasures were far outweighed by the never-ending barbarism—whippings, sometimes to death; loved ones sold and sent away, never to be seen again; physical torture of all kinds, even roasting human beings over a fire; the nightly rape of women and young girls.

Slaves had to fear their masters and occasionally the wives of their masters. The one thing slaves usually did not suffer from was a lack of food. They were generally well-fed since inadequately nourished slaves did not work well.

On January 1, 1863, President Lincoln issued the Emancipation Proclamation, declaring "that all persons held as slaves" in the secession states "are, and henceforward shall be free." Slavery could still exist in those border states that had not seceded, but Florida slaves were free, and as federal troops won more territory, that freedom expanded, freeing even more.

Most of the big Civil War battles took place outside the state, but in February 1864, Florida's largest battle was fought. A band of Confederate troops learned that Union troops aimed to retake Jacksonville before moving westward in an attempt to disrupt the transportation of food as well as cotton, timber, and other supplies. The Confederates set out to disrupt the Union plans. At the small town of Olustee west of Jacksonville, in a narrow passageway between a lake and a swamp, the Confederates had requested and obtained additional troops. They won the battle and delivered one of the highest casualty counts of the war, but the losses they experienced were almost as great.

Another battle, the last of any importance in Florida, happened a month later when a federal naval fleet transported Union troops to the coast south of Tallahassee. The Confederate troops won a victory, but it would be their last.

President Lincoln, fearing that the Emancipation Proclamation would be considered a temporary war measure, supported an amendment to the United States Constitution to officially abolish and prohibit slavery in the entire nation. That measure, the Thirteenth Amendment, was adopted in 1865.

There was little good news as anti-war feelings grew in Florida. Outspoken "loyal Confederate" governor John Milton was responsible for one more bit of shocking bad news being delivered to Confederate citizens when, sick and depressed, he committed suicide.

Just a few weeks later, on April 9, 1865, Gen. Robert E. Lee surrendered to the Union commander, Ulysses S. Grant, at Appomattox Court House, Virginia.

Because of its remoteness, the state capital at Tallahassee remained under Confederate control for another month before a U.S. flag was raised overhead. Florida, unlike the other former Confederate states, had minimal damage from the few battles fought there, so little rebuilding was necessary. Still, while there were celebrations, a way of life had ended. And sadly, the life of President Abraham Lincoln soon ended, too.

*Sketch showing the positions of the beacons
on the Florida reefs erected by Lieut. James Totten,
U.S. Army, Assistant, U.S.C.S.—
U.S. Coast Survey (1861)*

The extensive shallow coral reefs off Florida's coasts stretch from near Stuart, all the way to the Dry Tortugas, making the seas there dangerous for ships. The first fixed markers installed to indicate shallow water to sailors were day beacons, usually an upside down barrel on a pole, which was sometimes made of iron, with the barrel marked with numbers or letters. Because these were not visible at night, lighthouses were built in 1820 at Cape Florida, Sand Key, and the Dry Tortugas. In the extremely dangerous water six miles off Key Largo, the Carysfort Reef Light began operating in 1852.

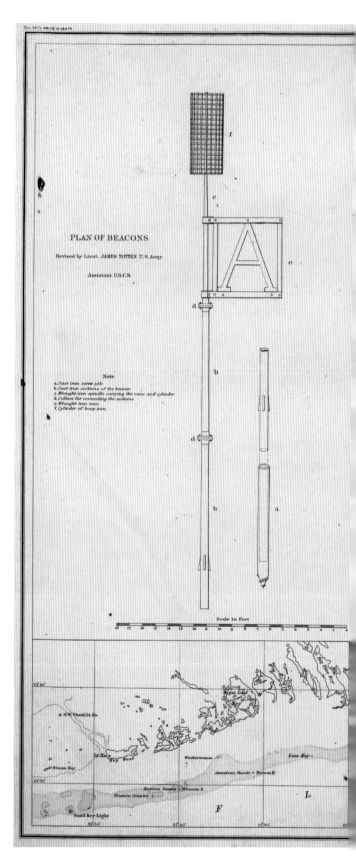

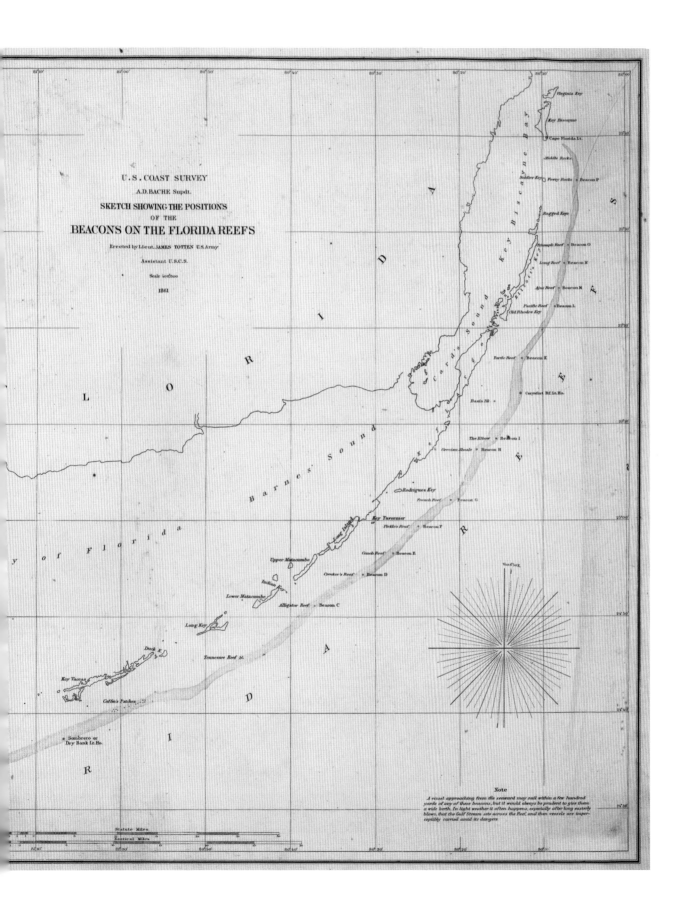

U.S. COAST SURVEY

A.D. BACHE Supdt.

SKETCH SHOWING THE POSITIONS

OF THE

BEACONS ON THE FLORIDA REEFS

Erected by Lieut. JAMES TOTTEN U.S.Army

Assistant U.S.C.S.

Scale 1/400000

1861

Note

A vessel approaching from the seaward may sail within a few hundred yards of any of these beacons, but it would always be prudent to give them a wide berth. In light weather it often happens, especially after long easterly blows, that the Gulf Stream sets across the Reef, and then vessels are imperceptibly carried amid its dangers

Statute Miles

Nautical Miles

*Birds eye view of Florida and part of Georgia
and Alabama   Bachmann (ca. 1861)*

Entitled *Panorama of the Seat of War*, this lithograph was
done by John Bachmann, a Swiss-born lithographer and
artist who became well known for his bird's-eye views.
This is one in a series he produced during the Civil War.

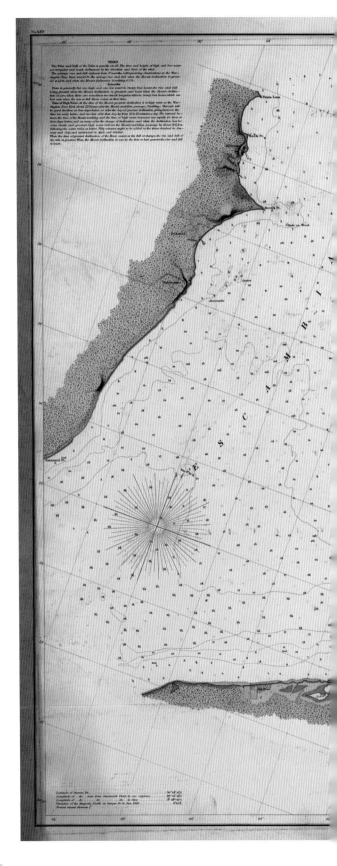

Preliminary chart of Escambia and Santa Maria de Galvaez [i.e., East] Bays, Florida. From a trigonometrical survey under the direction of A. D. Bache, Superintendent of the survey of the coast of the United States. Triangulation and topography by F. H. Gerdes, Asst. Hydrography by the party under the command of Lieut. Comdg. T. S. Phelps. U.S.N. Assist.—U. S. Coast Survey (1861)

The previous name of Pensacola Bay, Santa Maria de Galvez Bay, honored an officer in the Spanish militia who supported U.S. forces in fighting Great Britain during the Revolutionary War. Escambia Bay connects to the Gulf of Mexico by way of Pensacola Bay.

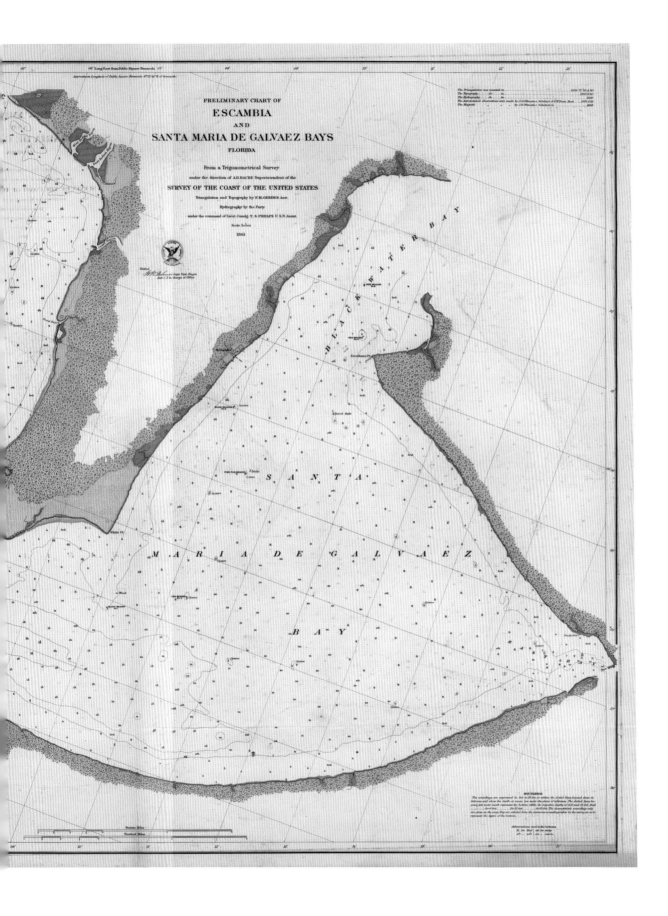

PRELIMINARY CHART OF

ESCAMBIA
AND
SANTA MARIA DE GALVAEZ BAYS
FLORIDA

From a Trigonometrical Survey
under the direction of A.D.BACHE Superintendent of the
SURVEY OF THE COAST OF THE UNITED STATES
Triangulation and Topography by F.H.GERDES Asst.
Hydrography by the Party
under the command of Lieut. Comdg. T. S. PHELPS U.S.N. Assist.

Scale 1⁄50000

1861

BLACKWATER BAY

SANTA

MARIA DE GALVAEZ

BAY

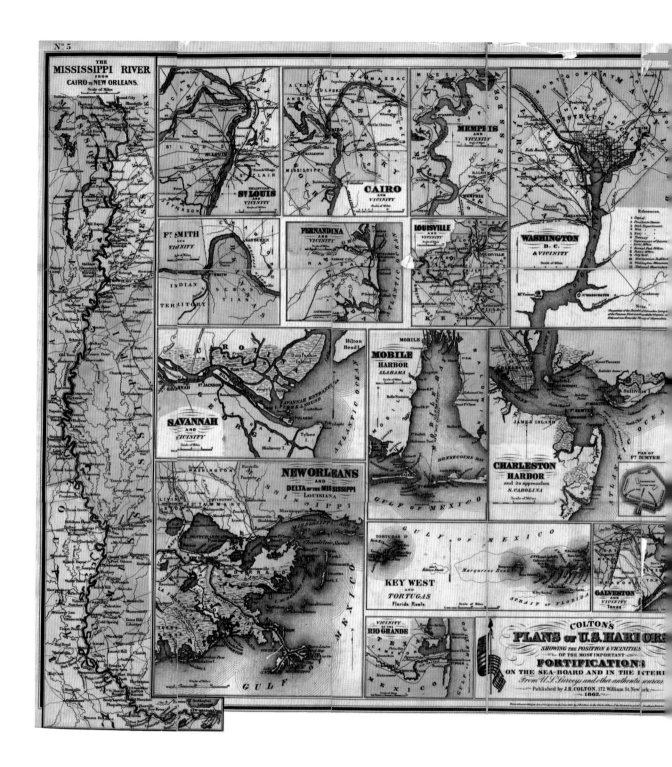

Colton's plans of U.S. harbors showing the position & vicinities of the most important fortifications on the sea-board and in the interior. From U.S. surveys and other authentic sources.—Colton (1862)

The twenty-three maps here show Fernandina Beach at the extreme northeastern border of Florida, Key West and the Tortugas at the farthest end of the Keys, and the entrance to Pensacola Bay in the Panhandle.

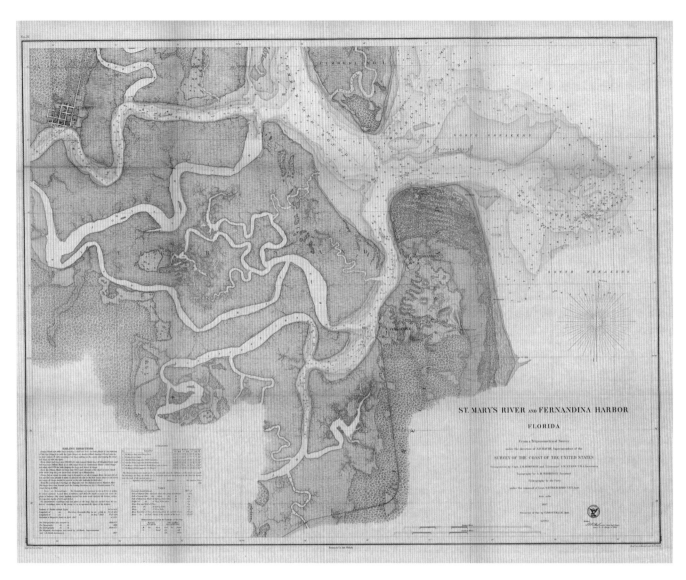

St. Mary's River and Fernandina harbor, Florida. From a trigonometrical survey under the direction of A. D. Bache, Superintendent of the survey of the coast of the United States. Triangulation by Capt. J. H. Simpson and Lieutenant A. W. Evans, U.S.A. Assistants. Topography by A. M. Harrison, Assistant. Hydrography by the party under the command of Lieut. S. D. Trenchard, U.S.N. Assist. 1857. Resurvey of bar by C. O. Boutelle, Asst. in 1862. Redd. drng. by P. Witzel. Engd. by A. Maedel and R. F. Bartle. Bowen & Co. lith., Philada.—U.S. Coast Survey (1862)

The growing town of Fernandina at the St. Marys River on the most northeastern border was captured by Union forces in 1863 and remained under their control until the end of the war.

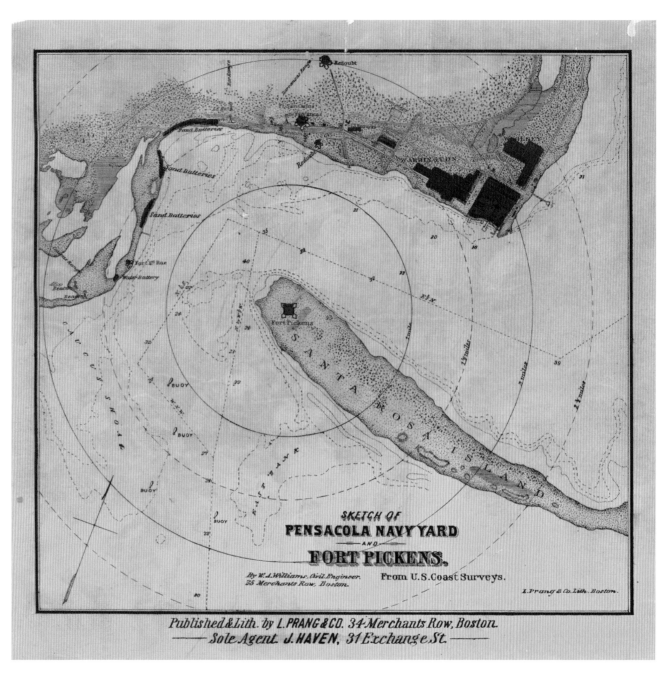

Sketch of Pensacola Navy Yard and Fort Pickens from U.S. coast surveys—Williams (186-)

Before the Civil War began at Fort Sumter in the Charleston harbor in 1861, Union forces had nominal control of Fort Pickens at Pensacola Bay, but strengthened their hold on that valuable site for the duration of the war.

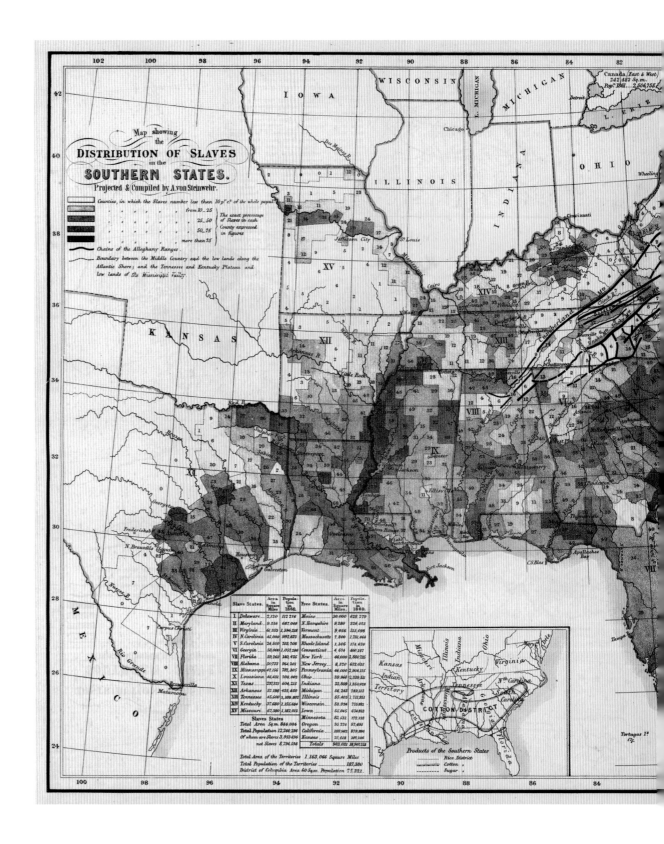

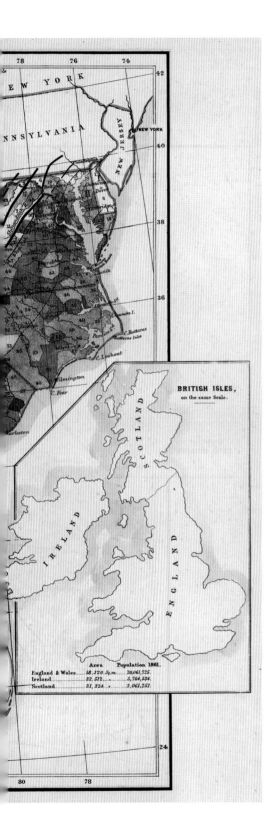

Map showing the distribution of slaves in the Southern States—
Steinwehr (186-)

Prior to the American Revolution, slavery existed in all British colonies in North America. Until the Thirteenth Amendment to the U.S. Constitution was ratified in 1865, slavery for life was legal throughout the country. Slaves were thought to be necessary where large plantations required field hands to raise valuable crops, such as cotton or sugar.

Drew's new map of the state of Florida, showing the townships by the U.S. Surveys, the completed &
projected railroads, the different railroad stations and growing railroad towns. The new towns on the rivers
and interior, and the new counties, up to the year 1874.

The Florida Rail Road, shown here, the state's only railroad running across the peninsula from Fernandina to
Cedar Key, was built by David Levy Yulee. He was one of the state's first two senators after Florida became a state
in 1845.

Industrialization

OF ALL THE DEFEATED CONFEDERATE STATES, Florida was the least impaired by the war. After a period of understandable confusion, the state government bounced back and economic growth and development followed. An exception to the prosperous times was the status of life for former slaves. They could call themselves free, but their lives remained extremely difficult.

The new Florida government followed the lead of other former secession states in its treatment of freed blacks, determined to keep them second-class citizens despite passage of the Freedmen's Bureau Bill in 1865. The bill helped find homes, food, hospitals, schools, and jobs for former slaves, but it could not prevent enactment of a poll tax, which effectively disenfranchised them, nor did it stop masked riders from terrorizing black communities.

The U.S. presidential election of 1876 was, at the time, the most contentious in the nation's history. New York's Samuel Tilden defeated Ohio's Rutherford B. Hayes in the popular vote and had a lead in the electoral vote by 184 to 165, with 20 uncounted votes in Florida, Louisiana, and South Carolina. After a prolonged battle, Hayes was declared the winner, but it was the bitterest of victories, with Florida's involvement an unbeknownst foreshadowing of the 2000 presidential election.

In the last decades of the century, reconstruction continued to elude southern parts of the state, with much of them remaining undeveloped wilderness, but signs of economic life blossomed in central Florida. Citrus grove owners and cattle ranchers saw their businesses expand to northern markets and to Cuba. The sale of timber and winter vegetables increased. Low taxes enticed some blacks as well as whites to move into the state, and Florida's weather attracted people for health reasons or simply for the pleasure of it.

All of this made the need for good transportation more imperative. In 1881 Governor William Bloxham hammered out land sales that freed millions of acres for rail construction. Three men were chiefly responsible for the enormous increase in the miles of railroads in Florida.

William D. Chipley, a Confederate soldier twice wounded and later imprisoned during the Civil War, went on to build a rail line running from Pensacola to the Apalachicola River and across it. The rail line forged a connection with other major systems and went a long way toward resolving transportation problems for west Florida. Known as west Florida's Mr. Railroad, Chipley later entered politics.

Henry B. Plant, a railroad executive originally from Connecticut, became interested in Florida after taking a trip to the state with his ailing wife. By developing hotels, railroads, and later, steamship lines, Plant linked Tampa to Jacksonville and farther to Georgia and the rest of the nation.

Best known of the three railroad tycoons was Henry Flagler, a partner of John D. Rockefeller of the Standard Oil Company. He was said to possess a $50 million nest egg when he, too, visited Jacksonville hoping his wife's poor health would improve. It did not, and after her death, he remarried. During a trip to Florida with his second wife, Flagler was so enchanted with St. Augustine, this country's oldest city that he built a multimillion-dollar hotel there, the Hotel Ponce de León. To give his guests access to his hotel, he built a rail line, the beginning of the Florida East Coast Railway.

Seeking even warmer days, Flagler pushed farther south to Daytona, then on to Palm Beach, where he built a second multimillion-dollar hotel, the Royal Poinciana. When the mercury fell to the teens in December 1894, an enterprising Miami woman, Julia Tuttle, convinced Flagler to extend his railroad all the way down the peninsula. He didn't stop there. In what was called Flagler's Folly by some and a feat of engineering genius by others, he expanded his Florida East Coast Railway across the water and islands to reach Key West. Throughout his many endeavors, Flagler alone conceived of, owned, and was responsible for them all.

Florida's tobacco production was seriously damaged by several strikes within the cigar-making industry, which had set up in Key West following violent disruptions among Cuban workers. A prominent leader in the industry, Vicente Martinez Ybor, chose Tampa as the new home for his cigar production, a sizable economic consideration. Not only was it a financial coup, but the boost to the ethnicity of the Tampa Bay population was also considerable. Closer ties to Cuba were formed, since most Floridians sympathized with Cubans in their desire for freedom from Spain.

A St. Johns riverboat pilot and sheriff of Duval County, Napoleon B. Broward was famed for running arms to Cuban rebels in his tugboat. He would later use his popularity to be elected governor of the state. Most Floridians agreed with Broward, sympathized with Cuban rebels, and wanted the United States to intervene.

In January 1898 President William McKinley reluctantly sent the battleship *Maine* to Havana, ninety miles from Florida, hoping this show of force might convince Spain to free Cuba. Mysteriously, the *Maine* exploded in Havana's harbor, with the loss of many American lives. The United States seemed to have no choice but to declare war on Spain.

The war lasted just four months. When a peace treaty was signed, the United States gained the Philippines, Guam, and Puerto Rico. Cuba fell under U.S. jurisdiction before forming its own government in 1902. The United States also acquired a perpetual lease on the area around Guantánamo Bay.

During the last twenty years of the nineteenth century, Floridians, realizing the necessity of overcoming their low literacy rate, set out to improve the state's poor education structure. Teachers were re-examined, more schools were built, and the school year was lengthened. Separate black schools opened in Tallahassee and Gainesville. Financially, it was a struggle but a necessary one. Several colleges also opened their doors, along with some small, private schools, including Rollins, Stetson, and Daytona's Bethune-Cookman College, which Mary McLeod Bethune had begun as a school for six black children.

Increased government spending, including the cost of housing for convicted criminals, compounded financial problems for the state. Florida attempted to solve that difficulty with the convict leasing system, whereby convicts sentenced for longer than a year were leased to private contractors, rarely with oversight by prison personnel. Contractors then paid the criminal's "salaries" to the state. Hard manual labor under atrocious conditions was the rule, and the inhumanity of it caught the attention of a young reporter, Mar-

jory Stoneman Douglas. She was inspired to write a poem about the system, garnering considerable attention to it and contributing to its demise.

As the century drew to a close, Florida suffered several disasters. Record-low temperatures in 1886 and 1895 caused severe financial losses. Sporadic yellow fever outbreaks in various counties, with a particularly virulent one in Jacksonville in 1888, resulted in more than four hundred deaths. Something good did follow, however. In an attempt to improve the handling of epidemics and other health matters, the State Board of Public Health was established in 1889 in Jacksonville.

Rapid growth and development in Florida, especially in the last half of the century, changed the face of the state. No longer a wilderness, tourists flocked in. Swamplands were drained and made profitable. Businesses sprang up to compete with one another. Citrus groves expanded and became known worldwide for their products. A new century was on its way.

Maps showing the Florida Transit and Peninsula Rail Road and its connections—Colton & Co. (1882)

The Florida Rail Road ran its first train in 1861, but the line failed financially and was reorganized twice more before it became the Florida Transit Rail Road in 1881.

Florida: Mapping the Sunshine State through History

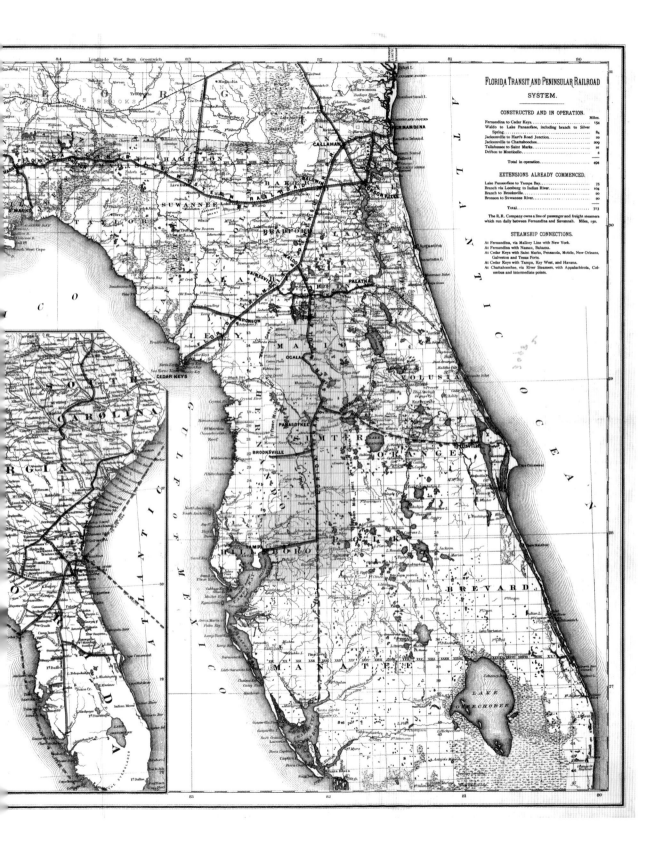

FLORIDA TRANSIT AND PENINSULAR RAILROAD
SYSTEM.

CONSTRUCTED AND IN OPERATION.

	Miles.
Fernandina to Cedar Keys.	154
Waldo to Lake Panasofkee, including branch to Silver Spring	84
Jacksonville to Hart's Road Junction	22
Jacksonville to Chattahoochee	209
Tallahassee to Saint Marks	21
Drifton to Monticello	4
Total in operation	494

EXTENSIONS ALREADY COMMENCED.

Lake Panasofkee to Tampa Bay	75
Branch via Leesburg to Indian River	104
Branch to Brooksville	20
Bronson to Suwannee River	20
Total	713

The R.R. Company owns a line of passenger and freight steamers which run daily between Fernandina and Savannah. Miles, 190.

STEAMSHIP CONNECTIONS.

At Fernandina, via Mallory Line with New York.
At Fernandina with Nassau, Bahama.
At Cedar Keys with Saint Marks, Pensacola, Mobile, New Orleans, Galveston and Texas Ports.
At Cedar Keys with Tampa, Key West, and Havana.
At Chattahoochee, via River Steamers, with Appalachicola, Columbus and intermediate points.

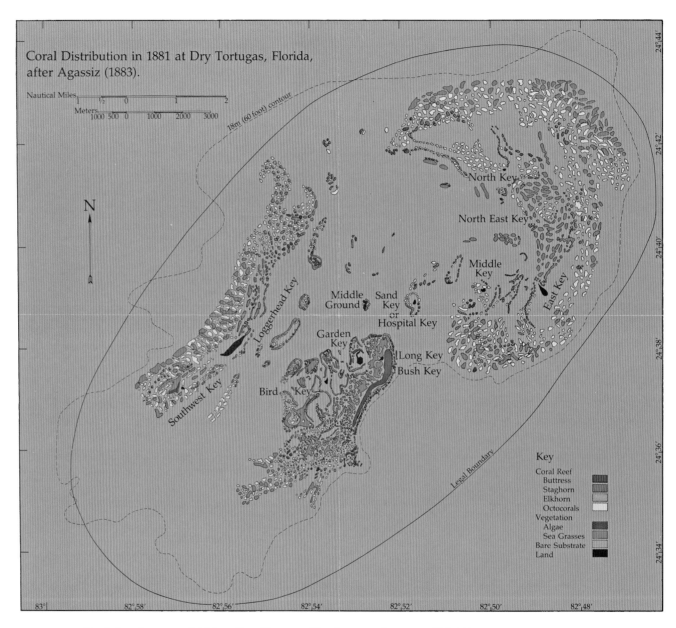

Coral Distribution in 1881 at Dry Tortugas, Florida, after Agassiz (1883).

Nautical Miles

Meters

18m (60 foot) contour

N

North Key

North East Key

Middle Key

Middle Ground

Sand Key or Hospital Key

East Key

Loggerhead Key

Garden Key

Long Key

Bush Key

Bird Key

Southwest Key

Legal Boundary

Key
Coral Reef
  Buttress
  Staghorn
  Elkhorn
  Octocorals
Vegetation
  Algae
  Sea Grasses
Bare Substrate
Land

Coral distribution in 1881 at Dry Tortugas, Florida, after Agassiz—(1883)

Because of their remote location, the reefs at the Dry Tortugas are basically untouched by divers, boat wrecks, or other human activity. Alexander Agassiz, a naturalist who made his observations while spending five weeks on a steam launch in 1881, produced this high-quality map of coral reefs. Monroe County, the southernmost county in the United States, includes part of the mainland and the islands of the Florida Keys. The county seat is Key West, where the cigar-making industry flourished before moving to Ybor City in Tampa in the 1880s.

Bird's eye view of Key West, Fla., Key West Island—Stoner (1884)

Key West, an island four miles long and two miles wide, with the Atlantic Ocean on one side and the Gulf of Mexico on the other, naturally attracted commercial fishermen, adventurous tourists, divers, the military, and wreck salvagers. Some of the "wreckers" were known to secretly rearrange channel markers, providing themselves with wrecks they could work when money was scarce.

Less than twenty years after Florida became a state, Key West was its largest city.

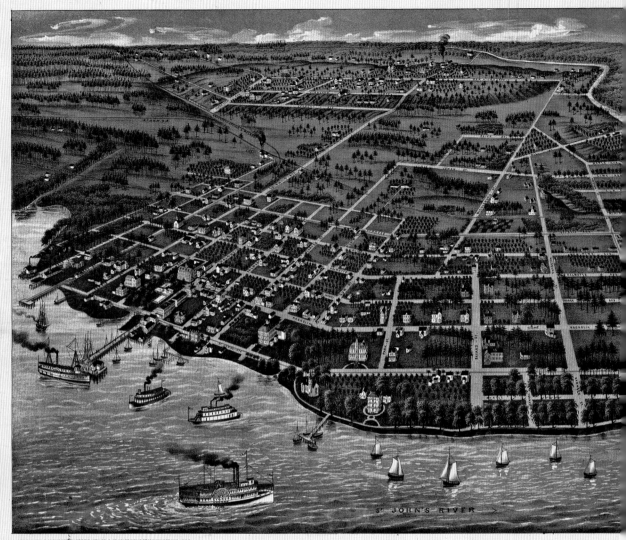

1 Episcopal Church.
2 Presbyterian Church.
3 Methodist Church.
4 Catholic Church.
5 Baptist Church.
6 African M. E. Church.
7 Colored Baptist Church.
8 County Court House and Jail.
9 School.
10 The Spring Office.

11 Post Office
12 Spring and Bath Pools.
13 Depots.
14 Street Railway Stables.
15 The Pines Hotel.
16 Clarendon Hotel, Harris and Applegate.
17 The Morganza, A. G. Morgan Proprietor.
18 The Riverside.
19 Magnolia Hotel.
20 Crocker's Hall.
21 Saw, Planing and Shingle Mills.

ST. JOHN'S RIVER →

GREEN COVE SP
COUNTY SEAT OF CLAY COUNTY
FLORIDA.
1885.

The 30th parallel of North latitude crosses Clay County, Florida, somewhat north of the center, and just south of the parallel on the west bank of the St. Johns river lies the town of Green Cove Springs, the county seat, one of the most popular and widely known winter resorts in Florida. Its famous sulphur spring has drawn people from every land and clime to bathe in and drink of its healing waters. Encircling the chasm whence the famous fountain flows, the town has grown beyond the encampment of the dusky Seminole, until it now embraces an area of about two square miles and contains six churches, three public schools, six hotels, a number of stores, two saw-mills and a manufactory of shingles. Its resident population is about one thousand, cosmopolitan in character, and generally genial and friendly in disposition. The transportation facilities are unsurpassed in any town in Florida; three large piers jutting out into the St. Johns, affords convenient access to sea-going vessels and river craft of every kind, while the Jacksonville, Tampa and Key West Railroad, running through the center of the town gives communication with the railroad systems of the country. The town is also the terminus of the Green Cove Springs and Melrose Railroad, which is now in operation for a distance of twelve miles, and is intended to cross the peninsula. Another through line of railroad, affording direct communication with other railroad systems, is partly constructed, and when it shall be completed, Green Cove Springs will have two competitive paralell lines of railroad. Through some of the principal streets of the town, a line of street railroad has recently been completed and is now in operation, connecting with all the railroad stations, wharfs and hotels.

The tract of land on which the town of Green Cove Springs is built, is known as the "Bayard Tract," fronting on the St. Johns river for some fourteen miles, (the larger part

of which is now in market,) is one of
who was at the time Surveyor General
Clinch, then in command of the army i
bluff hammock, fronting on the St. Jo
fifty feet above the tide water. A few
course to the north just below the corp
on the St. Johns. Commencing one ha
of decay. Much of the surface is a dar
These marl lands have been found to
large annual expense usually incurred i
portation, our many hotels and boarding
settlers who come to Florida hoping to

BECK & PAULI, Litho, Milwaukee, Wis.

NGS.

This tract, during the time that Florida was a Spanish colony, was granted by the government to G. I. F. Clark, [in] position he had every chance for choosing the best. Shortly after the United States purchased Florida, Gen. [bou]ght this tract of land from Don Clark, and it has remained in his family every since. It has miles of the best [fr]om the river it is diversified by creeks and ridges, some of the ridges rising to a height of one hundred and [fi]ve Springs, the river turns from its general course and runs nearly due west as far as the town, again taking its [g]ives many miles of river lands protected on the north by twenty miles of water, the best water protection [riv]er, there is a large body of land underlaid with shell marl, the shell being largely mixed with bones in all stages [it] is admirably suited to truck-growing, producing more to a given area than any other class of land in the State. [o]range and other fruit culture; the marl furnishing all needed elements for their rapid growth, thus saving the [com]mercial fertilizers. For vegetable growing, our rich low lands abundant marl deposits our facilities for trans-[port] and cheap communication to all important points, make Clay county a very desirable locality for that class of [the] products of the soil. For further information address C. C. BEMIS. G. C. S, Florida.

Green Cove Springs, county seat of Clay County, Florida—Beck & Pauli (1885)
First called White Sulfur Springs and renamed about 1850, Green Cove Springs attracted tourists who came by steamboat on the St. Johns River for the healing properties of the spring's sulfur water.

Jacksonville, Florida—Koch (1893)

Jacksonville was a favorite winter resort for the rich during the Gilded Age following the Civil War. However, tourism there declined after Henry Flagler extended the Florida East Coast Railway south to Miami in 1896. Yellow fever epidemics in 1886 and 1888 had also contributed to the town's decline.

JACKSONVILLE
FLORIDA.

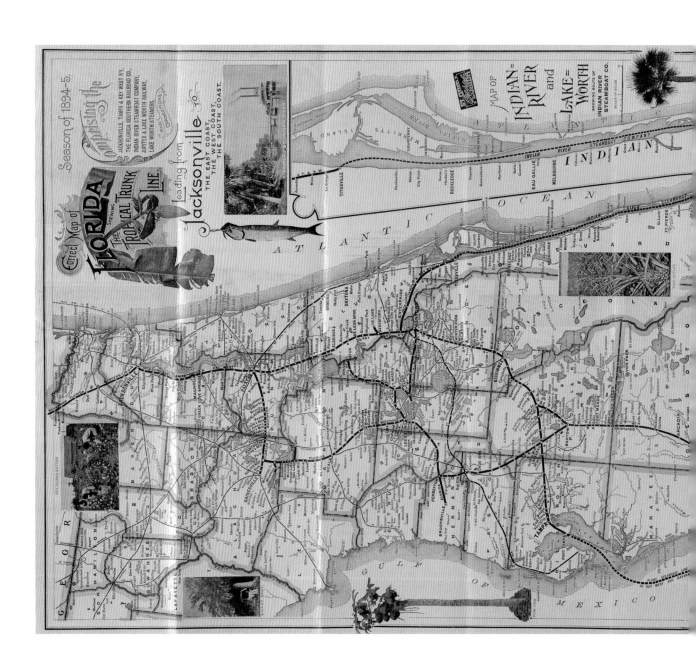

Correct map of Florida, season of 1894–5; showing the Tropical Trunk Line, comprising the Jacksonville, Tampa & Key West R'y, the Florida Southern Railroad Co., Indian River Steamboat Company, Jupiter & Lake Worth Railway, Lake Worth steamers, and connections: leading from Jacksonville to the east coast, the west coast, the south coast—Matthews-Northrup Co. (1894)

The Tropical Trunk Line extended from Jacksonville to the east coast, the west coast and the south coast. In 1895, when Henry Flagler extended his Florida East Coast Railway to Palm Beach, the keen competition forced some smaller railroads out of business.

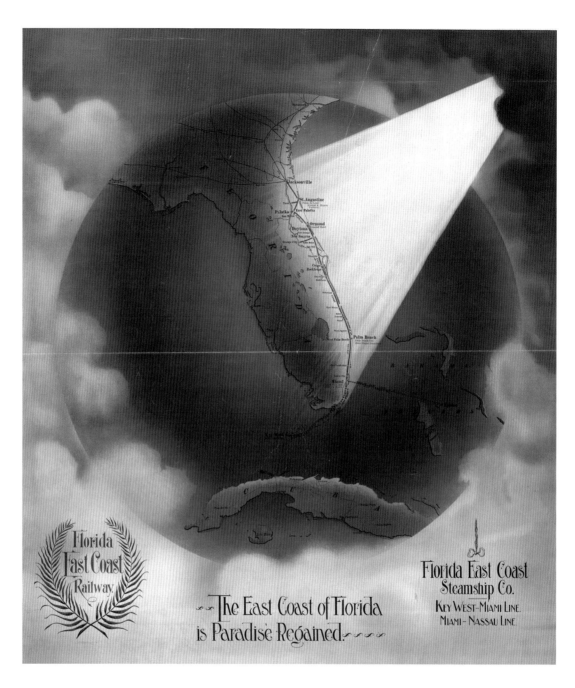

The east coast of Florida is paradise regained—Beckwith (1898)

This 1898 image assures the viewer that paradise may be found by patronizing the Florida East Coast Railway and the Florida East Coast Steamship Company, all the way from Jacksonville to Key West.

Twentieth and Twenty-first Centuries

IT WAS A NEW CENTURY AND A NEW FLORIDA. Citrus groves moved to the south central part of the state after the 1894–95 freeze, and developers followed. More people needed more room and more roads and more housing. Retirees were attracted not only to the sunshine but also to lower taxes and a lower cost of living. New communities seemed to spring up overnight.

While railroad miles expanded dramatically, automobiles came on the scene and Florida loved them. New car owners paid a $2 yearly fee to help build roads to drive on. Carmaker Carl Fisher introduced exciting car racing on the hard Daytona Beach sand in 1903.

World War I erupted in Europe in 1914, but under President Woodrow Wilson, the United States tried to remain neutral. By 1917, when German submarine attacks on American ships made that impossible, the United States declared war on Germany and Florida rose to the challenge.

Her good weather brought five of the thirty-five U.S. flight schools to Florida; the most highly regarded was in Pensacola. Tampa and Jacksonville boasted huge shipyards. Thomas Edison had a workshop for depth bombs at the naval training base at Key West, where there was also a submarine headquarters.

The civilian population got busy as well, increasing shipments of turpentine, lumber, phosphates, oranges, and various vegetables to where they were needed. Many black Floridians found good-paying jobs for the first time, but others left the state to move north where they found more freedom.

Floridians rejoiced when the Armistice was signed in 1918, before another major upheaval called Prohibition went into effect. Florida had mostly been a conservative state, but the impact of the new law was far-reaching. A couple thousand miles of shoreline and proximity to the Caribbean islands made it inevitable that Florida would be a major port of entry for smugglers. Native Florida Crackers, "moonshiners" from early times, appreciated this new opportunity.

The legislature, meanwhile, tempted even more people to relocate to Florida by amending the constitution to bar income and inheritance taxes.

As people poured in, mostly by packed cars, the state badly needed more roads. By 1923 Florida had her first concrete highway, between Lake City and Jacksonville. Soon, the Tamiami Trail opened from Miami to Fort Myers, along with other important north-south routes. Airplanes, too, became popular, so that by 1926 Florida had nine airports for travelers flying into the Sunshine State.

South Florida boomed. Carl Fisher influenced construction of the long north-south Dixie Highway, connecting the Midwest and Florida, then built a whole island and called it Miami Beach. George Merrick developed Coral Gables, featuring a swimming pool cut from coral rock that became famous as the Venetian Pool. To the north Addison Mizner developed Palm Beach, where homes had pink walls and red tile roofs, and some had solid gold doorknobs. Miami itself was a chaos of real estate agents and folks looking for real estate bargains.

Then in 1926, a hurricane with 125-mile-per-hour winds hit the area. Hundreds of lives were lost, with thousands of homes destroyed, boats stuck on dry land, and cars washed out to sea. Two years later, another hurricane hit closer to Palm Beach, and the boom became a bust. People left in droves, real estate collapsed, and Florida sank into a bottomless depression.

While whites had enjoyed the boom years, blacks did not experience an accompanying prosperity. In 1923 one of the worst human-rights violations in the nation's history occurred while white men raced cars at Daytona and bathing beauties cavorted on Miami beaches. The U.S. commitment to "make the world safe for democracy" did not include African Americans.

On January 5 a white woman claimed to have been assaulted by a black man in her Rosewood home. Her story was suspicious, but news spread quickly and an ugly mob swarmed. The few blacks who weren't slaughtered hid, terrified, in nearby icy swamps. The following day, the bloodthirsty horde finished burning homes in Rosewood to the ground. The peaceful town was gone, but an ugly stain scarred the Sunshine State.

In 1929 Florida joined the rest of the country in suffering the Great Depression. With no easy fixes, the Works Progress Administration (WPA), under President Franklin D. Roosevelt stepped in. Men were employed building new levees around Lake Okeechobee to prevent flooding. Building badly needed bridges, schools, roads, and post offices provided jobs for heads of families. Under the Federal Writers' Project, unemployed writers found jobs, including Zora Neale Hurston, whose *Their Eyes Were Watching God* and other books are now considered classics. Zora, who grew up in Eatonville, Florida, created a guide of the state as part of the Federal Writers' Project. Because of her race, Zora had to accept an inferior position to less-qualified whites, but at least she was employed.

At the start of the 1940s, cigar production at Ybor City surged. The sponge industry at nearby Tarpon Springs was going well. Likewise, Plant City strawberries were shipped in great quantities, a phosphate industry showed promise, and paper production in the Panhandle was up.

Florida's clear skies convinced the U.S. military to launch training bases at Orlando, Jacksonville, Miami, and Arcadia. The base at Pensacola was expanded, and MacDill, a new base at Tampa, was constructed. Eglin Air Force Base, located in the Panhandle at Valparaiso, would one day become the largest air force base in the world.

On December 7, 1941, the entire country's attention turned to World War II.

Florida's skies seemed full of airplanes. Offshore, German submarines attempted to prevent supplies being sent to Europe by torpedoing merchant ships. Horrified beachgoers watched explosions a few miles offshore. Civilians volunteered as spotters to relay reports of any activity in the air or ocean.

When the war ended in 1945, huge numbers of veterans who had been stationed in Florida during the war remembered the ocean, the beaches, and the climate, and they returned with their families to make homes. Florida's population surged once more, at levels great enough to concern environmentalists, Marjory Stoneman Douglas among them.

Though there was peace, it was not a peaceful time. The Cold War with the Soviet Union had begun.

The Missile Test Center, near Cape Canaveral, was already testing rockets over the Atlantic Ocean when, in 1957, the Soviet Union launched *Sputnik*, the first earth-orbiting satellite. With that, the Space Race began, setting American nerves on edge. The center at the Cape became the National Aeronautics and Space Administration, and Brevard County, where it was located, boomed and continued to boom to four times its size within ten years.

Another extraordinary real estate upheaval occurred in 1971 when Disney World, a tourist attraction unlike any other, opened near Orlando. In its first two years of operation, $3 billion was taken in at the gate.

In 1980 Cuba's leader, Fidel Castro, allowed 130,000 citizens to leave for Florida in the Mariel Boatlift, but he secretly included criminals and mental patients, straining social services in the area to the breaking point and forcing President Jimmy Carter to declare a state of emergency.

Many Florida citizens were embarrassed by the inept handling of their part in the presidential election of 2000, and they felt their skin crawl again in 2001. The horror of the bombing of the World Trade Center in New York was terrifying enough, but to hear that several of the terrorists responsible had trained in Florida flight schools curdled their blood.

The former paradise felt tainted. There were too many people, not enough money, too much concrete, wetlands disappearing, native plants and animals becoming extinct, and on and on. Will it stop, Florida wondered? When?

*Panoramic view of West Palm Beach,
North Palm Beach, and Lake Worth—
Pleuthner (1915)*
Looking west from the Atlantic Ocean, North Palm Beach, developed by J. D. MacArthur, comes into view, then West Palm Beach, founded by Henry Flagler as a place for his hotel workers to live, and finally Lake Worth, named for the lake along its border.

EVERGLADES

NORTH PALM BEACH

LAKE WORTH

ATLANTIC OCEAN

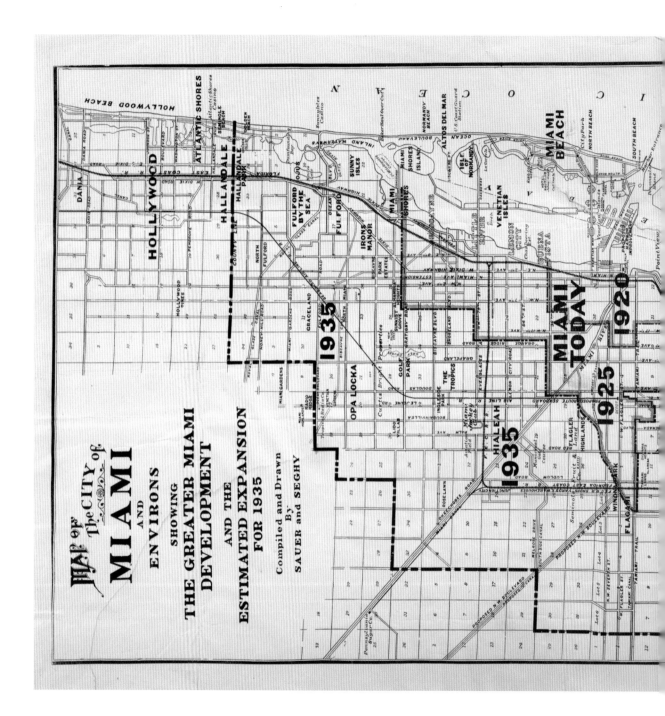

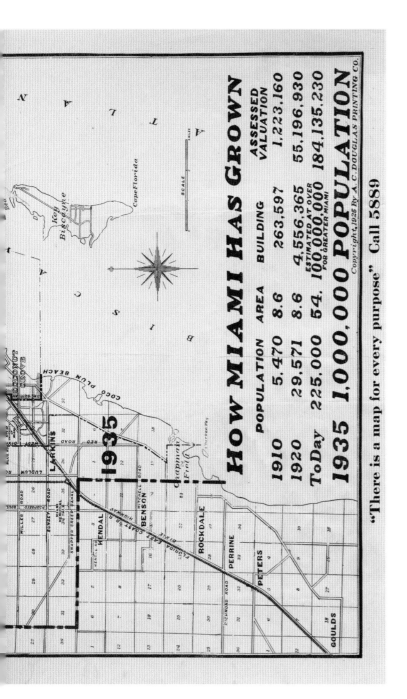

Map of the city of Miami and Environs showing the greater Miami Development and estimated expansion for 1935— Sauer and Seghy (1936)

Home to all of three hundred residents when incorporated as a city in 1896, Miami grew at a breathtaking pace to become a well-known global city, important in international finance, entertainment, culture, and the arts.

Aero—View of
TALLAHASSEE
1926

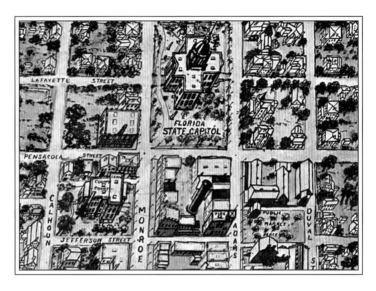

Aero-view of Tallahassee—Wynne (1926)

The boom of the early 1920s began to slow in 1925, and with it, Florida's golden reputation began to lose its glow. Tallahassee escaped the ravages of the great 1926 hurricane that so devastated Dade County, but economic hard times spread throughout Florida as well as the rest of the United States.

World Famous Resorts on the East Coast of Florida. East Coast Railway—J. W. Clement Co.-Matthews-Northrup Works (1929)

After building the multimillion-dollar Ponce de Léon Hotel in St. Augustine, Henry Flagler constructed a railroad to transport hotel guests from Jacksonville in comfort. Seeking even more tropical temperatures, he then continued his railroad farther south to Palm Beach where he established two more luxury hotels, the Royal Poinciana and the Breakers. Eventually, at Julia Tuttle's urging, he extended the railway all the way to Miami where he opened the Royal Palm Hotel.

The extension of Flagler's FEC Railway to Key West, the finest deep-water harbor south of Norfolk, Virginia, was completed when he rode the first train there in 1912.

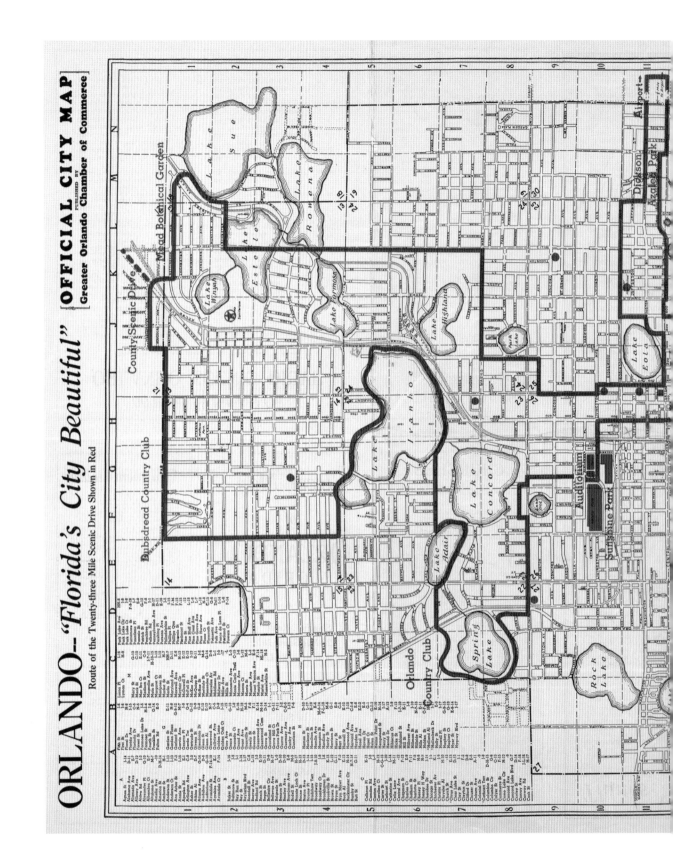

ORLANDO—"Florida's City Beautiful"

OFFICIAL CITY MAP

PUBLISHED BY
Greater Orlando Chamber of Commerce

Route of the Twenty-three Mile Scenic Drive Shown in Red

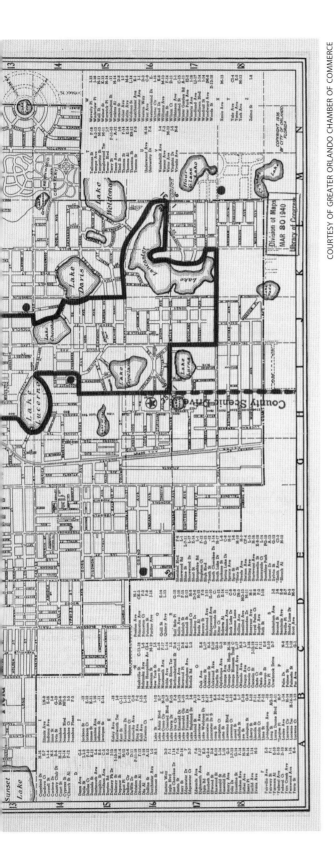

Orlando, Florida's Beautiful City. Official City Map—
Greater Orlando Chamber of Commerce (1936)

Orlando, the county seat of Orange County, was originally the center of the citrus industry, but following the Great Freeze of 1894–95, Florida's largest inland city began to evolve into a popular resort. Many ex-GIs who had been stationed there during World War II returned at the war's end to settle with their families. In 1971 Walt Disney World opened, followed by other theme parks, ushering in a dramatic rise in tourism and a steady progression in the development of a major industrial and hi-tech center.

Florida—Prepared by Geography Division in cooperation with Data Preparation Division (1983)

Over the years, Florida's location allowed for a complex mixture of cultures and languages unlike any other area of the United States. From earliest times, people from everywhere met in the subtropical peninsula, but following World War II, Florida's population exploded with 13 million newcomers arriving between 1950 and 2000. The number of Hispanics more than doubled, starting with Cubans, joined by immigrants from Mexico, Peru, Nicaragua, Venezuela, and other Central and South American countries. They joined Native Americans, the descendants of Scots colonists in Sarasota, the Swedes in Sanford, Greeks in Tarpon Springs, Jews in Miami, Danes in St. Lucie County, and Bahamians in Key West, to form a vital, ever-changing, sometimes messy environment.

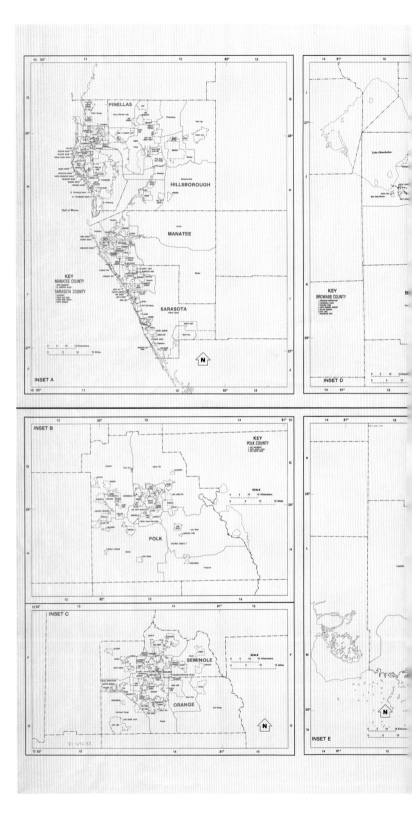

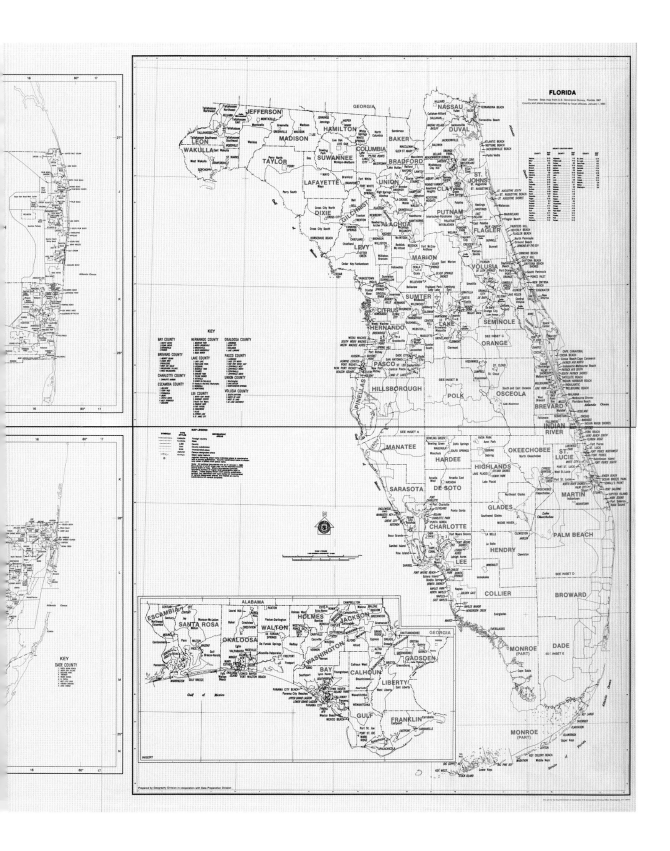

FLORIDA

Central America and the Caribbean—
Central Intelligence Agency (1990)
This map demonstrates the importance geography has played,
still plays, and will play, both good and bad, in the future narrative of the Sunshine State.

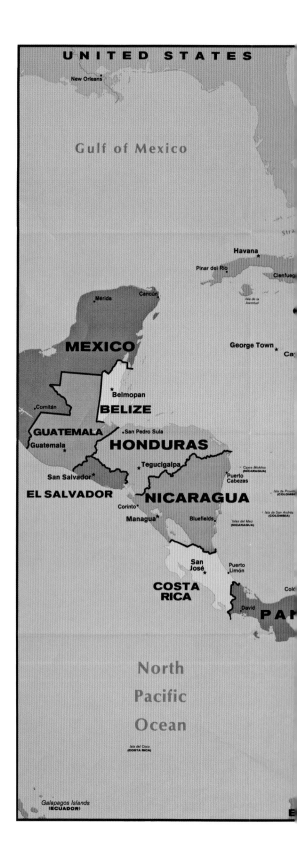

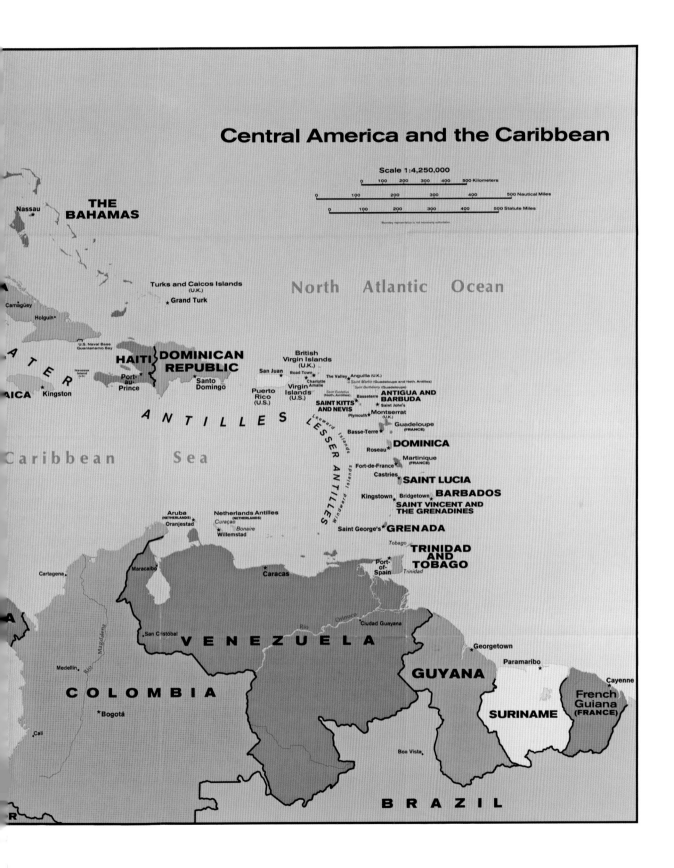

Central America and the Caribbean

Scale 1:4,250,000

0	100	200	300	400	500 Kilometers
0	100	200	300	400	500 Nautical Miles
0	100	200	300	400	500 Statute Miles

Boundary representation is not necessarily authoritative.

Nassau ★

THE BAHAMAS

Camagüey

Holguín ★

North   Atlantic   Ocean

Turks and Caicos Islands
(U.K.)
★ Grand Turk

U.S. Naval Base
Guantanamo Bay

HAITI

Navassa
Island
(U.S.)

Port-
au-
Prince ★

**DOMINICAN
REPUBLIC**

★ Santo
Domingo

San Juan ★

British
Virgin Islands
(U.K.)

Road Town
★

Charlotte
Amalie

Anguilla (U.K.)
The Valley ★

Saint Martin (Guadeloupe and Neth. Antilles)
Saint Barthélemy (Guadeloupe)

Puerto
Rico
(U.S.)

Virgin
Islands
(U.S.)

Saint Eustatius
(Neth. Antilles)

Basseterre
★

**ANTIGUA AND
BARBUDA**

**SAINT KITTS
AND NEVIS**

★ Saint John's

Plymouth ★

Montserrat
(U.K.)

GREATER

JAMAICA

Kingston ★

ANTILLES

Caribbean   Sea

Basse-Terre ★

Guadeloupe
(FRANCE)

Roseau ★

DOMINICA

Leeward Islands

LESSER ANTILLES

Fort-de-France ★

Martinique
(FRANCE)

Castries ★

SAINT LUCIA

Windward Islands

Kingstown ★

Bridgetown ★

BARBADOS

**SAINT VINCENT AND
THE GRENADINES**

Aruba
(NETHERLANDS)
Oranjestad ★

Netherlands Antilles
(NETHERLANDS)
Curaçao
★
Willemstad

Bonaire

Saint George's ★ **GRENADA**

Tobago

Port-
of-
Spain ★

**TRINIDAD
AND
TOBAGO**

Trinidad

Cartagena

Maracaibo

Caracas ★

Medellín

Rio Magdalena

V E N E Z U E L A

San Cristóbal

Rio *Orinoco*

Ciudad Guayana

Georgetown
★

Paramaribo
★

Cayenne
★

COLOMBIA

★ Bogotá

Cali

GUYANA

SURINAME

French
Guiana
(FRANCE)

Boa Vista

B R A Z I L

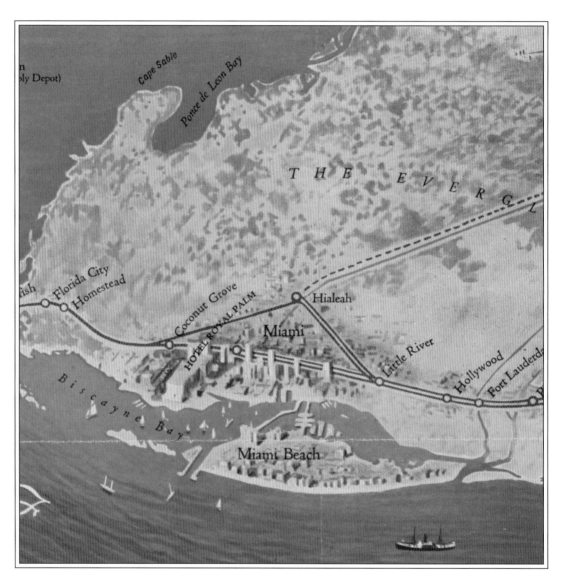

Detail from map on pages 102 and 103

Conclusion

ONCE TOTALLY SUBMERGED UNDER THE SEA, Florida's life and culture is and always has been more closely linked to water than any other part of the continent from which it protrudes. The peninsula's 1,200 miles of coastline alone would be sufficient to attract people, but from earliest times, Florida's 30,000 lakes of all sizes, 12,000 miles of rivers and streams, 4,500 islands, and at least 600 springs have drawn people from the rest of the world. Even thousands of feet underneath the state and extending into Georgia and South Carolina, there is water, 100,000 square miles of it, called the Florida Aquifer, which provides water for millions of people.

The unproveable myth persists that Ponce de León sailed over the sea from Puerto Rico looking for water—the Fountain of Youth—when he came upon this beautiful coast he named *Florida.* Ponce de Léon is also credited with discovering the warm, swift current of water flowing from the Gulf of Mexico through the Florida Straits, then following the eastern coast to Newfoundland before it crosses to Europe. We know it as the Gulf Stream.

Thanks in part to writer and environmentalist Marjory Stoneman Douglas, one of the most talked about areas of Florida wetlands now is the unique Everglades, 6,200 square miles of water renamed by her as the River of Grass. Spanish adventurers, encountering alligators, venomous snakes, dark swamps, and foggy marshes as they tried to explore Florida, had still another name for it. They called it the "Lagoon of the Sacred Spirit." In the early years, the Everglades, which covered most of south Florida, was so desolate and forbidding that it seemed preferable to observe it from a distance, and for the briefest time possible. However, after the Seminoles were defeated in a third war with white settlers, a few hundred of them disappeared into the Everglades to make their homes, relatively secure in the certainty that whites would have no desire to follow.

Florida can claim the second-largest freshwater lake within the continental United States—Lake Okeechobee, which covers 730 square miles. In the nineteenth century the lake was so packed with trout, bass, and catfish that fishermen claimed they didn't need fishing poles, because fish in the Big O, as it was sometimes called, jumped right into their boats. Following a hurricane in 1926 when three hundred people were killed, then another devastating hurricane in 1928 that killed nearly two thousand people, the

Army Corps of Engineers spent $100 million to encircle the lake with a twenty-foot-high dike. The Corps made it even higher in the 1960s.

The St. Johns River, Florida's longest river, is 310 miles long but only thirty feet deep. A lazy river, it flows at one third of a mile per hour and is one of the few U.S. rivers to flow north. It begins at Blue Cypress Lake in Indian River County and follows the coastline to join the Atlantic Ocean at Jacksonville. In the early days, steamships and paddle wheelers hauled cargo and visitors up and down the river. Replaced at first by railroads, then by highways, the St. Johns River so enchanted Harriet Beecher Stowe, author of *Uncle Tom's Cabin,* that she even allowed herself to be touted as a tourist attraction for a steamship line. As she worked on a book, she would wave from the porch of her home on the riverbank to tourists on passing ships.

Marjorie Kinnan Rawlings, author of *The Yearling* and *Cross Creek,* lived not at the edge of the river, but in central Florida in the heart of Florida Cracker country. She became enchanted with the St. Johns River when she and a friend explored part of it in an eighteen-foot boat, unprepared for the rough crossing they experienced on Lake George, one of the many lakes on this River of Lakes. Lake George, the second-largest lake in Florida, is shallow enough that it doesn't take much wind to make crossing it in a small boat an exciting experience, as Rawlings learned.

It's hard to believe that here, long ago, where the St. Johns River meets the ocean, the bustling city of Jacksonville was called Cow Ford, named because it was a shallower place where cows and other supplies could be safely crossed to the other side of the river. Now, ferries cross the river, and shrimp trawlers, private sailboats and powerboats,

and commercial tourist cruisers pass the nearby U.S. Coast Guard Station and the Naval Air Station, where dozens of guided-missile cruisers, destroyers, and guided-missile frigates are docked. The city of Jacksonville, county seat of Duval County, has attracted so much growth that it has taken over the entire bustling county. The writer Stephen Crane was less than charmed when he visited Jacksonville in the days after the Civil War. He was quoted as saying that Jacksonville "looks like soiled pasteboard that some lunatic babies have been playing with."

Among the thousands of Florida islands, none are more famous than the Florida Keys, which stretch through the water for two hundred miles, southwest from the tip of the peninsula to the Gulf of Mexico. Cigars, sponges, and canning factories figured prominently in their past, but as with the rest of the country, the islands were hard hit in the Great Depression. With a boost from author Ernest Hemingway, who wrote some of his famous novels when he made his home in Key West from 1928 to 1940, other writers and artists were drawn there, sparking an increase in tourism.

The importance of water to the state of Florida cannot be denied, whether it is the water that surrounds it for 1,200 miles, the water beneath it in the aquifer, or the water that falls from the heavens or floods in from the sea during a hurricane. Though it was what attracted people to the Sunshine State from earliest years, humans have always seemed to feel the need to control it. And control it they did—for a while.

The Army Corps of Engineers was enlisted to advance on the enemy, which was water in the wrong places. Dikes were built, rivers were straightened, canals were dug. Where before there was a River of Grass, now there were sugarcane fields. Where there had been sawgrass and swamp, now there were subdivisions. Where alligators and indigenous snakes had lived, now there were pythons and sinkholes. Before Florida knew it, eight million people were living in what used to be the wilderness, which had been turned into a managed environment.

Thousands of acres of fields and forests were replaced by condominiums. The state's famous orange groves were bulldozed to make way for strip malls and high-rise apartment buildings. Enormous amounts of sewage needed to be disposed of, with less space to do so, but developers didn't seem to care. The people who did care were outnumbered and less influential.

Marjory Stoneman Douglas would not take all the credit for arousing the public's attention to the frightening circumstances of the state's ecology. Even her father had expounded on its sad state in 1906, in the *Miami Herald*, of which he was its editor. Still, Marjory and her book, *The Everglades: River of Grass*, first published in 1947 and remaining a big seller, were hard to ignore. But it was only a beginning. As Marjory's often-quoted remark warned, "The Everglades is a test. If we pass, we get to keep the planet."

Work has begun. The absurdity of a proposed Jetport in the Everglades was killed, likewise the horror of a Cross Florida Barge Canal. The Army Corps of Engineers has started to undo the many years of the labors of its precursors. Some wetlands-restoration projects are under way throughout Florida. Others were felled by the Great Recession. There is more to do, much more. Is it too late?

Acknowledgments

First on the list is Erin Turner whose vision and creative editorial participation make these books a joy for me; without her this audacious project would not be the permanent achievement it is destined to be. On our Globe Pequot Press team I treasure Julie Marsh (indefatigable project editor), Sheryl Kober (visionary designer–Oh, these vellum jackets!), Lori Enik (digital file miracle worker), and Casey Shain (layout and Photoshop artist). The patience, organizational skills, and technical wizardry of my gifted colleague Aimee Hess are essential to my survival, as is the research assistance I receive from the masters in the Library of Congress Geography and Map Division: John Hebert (its Chief), Cynthia Cook, John Hessler, Charlotte Houtz, Michael Klein, Stephen Paczolt, and Edward Redmond.

—Vincent Virga

I am deeply grateful to Erin Turner and Julie Marsh for their wise and patient editorial guidance. Thanks to Wendy Wright for her support. Finally, thanks to Dr. George F. Wright, my guru and best friend.

—E. Lynne Wright

All maps come from the Library of Congress Geography and Map Division unless otherwise noted. To order reproductions of Library of Congress items, please contact the Library of Congress Photoduplication Service, Washington, D.C., 20540-4570 or (202) 707-5640.

Page viii Ruysch, Johann. "Universalior cogniti orbis tabula." In Claudius Ptolemeus, *Geographia.* Rome, 1507. G1005.1507 Vault.

Page ix Waldseemüller, Martin. "Universalis cosmographia secundum Ptholomaei traditionem et Americi Vespucii aloru[m] que lustrations," St. Dié, France?, 1507. G3200 1507.W3 Vault.

Pages 8–9 Florida with the march of de Soto and his men, 1539–1544. From the book *De Soto and his men in the land of Florida,* by Grace King, with illustrations by George Gibbs. New York: The Macmillan Company,1898. E125.S7.K5. General Collections, Library of Congress.

Pages 10–11 Santa Cruz, Alonso de. Mapa del Golfo y costa de la Nueva España: desde el Río de Panuco hasta el cabo de Santa Elena, 1572? G3860 1572 .S3 Vault : Low 60.

Pages 12–13 (detail, page ii) Ortelius, Abraham. Peruuiae avriferæ regionis typus. Didaco Mendezio auctore. La Florida, auctore Hieron. Chiaues. Guastecan reg., 1584. G3290 1584 .O7 Vault.

Pages 14–15 (detail, page 4) Boazio, Baptista. Map and views illustrating Sir Francis Drake's West Indian Voyage, 1585-6. London?, 1589. G3291.S12 s000 .B6.

Pages 16–17 Le Moyne de Morgues, Jacques. Floridae Americae provinciae recens & exactissima descriptio auctorè Iacobo le Moyne cui cognomen de Morgues, qui Laudūnierum, altera Gallorum in eam prouinciam nauigatione comitat est, atque adhibitis aliquot militibus ob pericula, regionis illius interiora & maritima diligentissimè lustrauit, & exactissimè dimensus est, obseruata

etiam singulorum fluminum inter se distantia, ut ipsemet redux Carolo .IX. Galliarum regi, demonstrauit, 1591. G3930 1591 .L4 Vault: Low 73.

Page 18 Bry, Theodor de. They reach Port Royal. Illus. in: Brevis narratio eorvm qvæ in Florida Americæ provïcia Gallis acciderunt,: secunda in illam nauigatione, duce Renato de Laudōniere ... anno MDLXIIII. Qvae est secvnda pars Americae ... Auctore Iacobo Le Moyne, cui cognomen de Morgues ... Nunc primùm Gallico sermone à Theodoro de Bry Leodiense in lucem edita: Latio verò donata a C. C. A. Francoforti ad Moenvm: Typis I. Wecheli, sumtibus vero T. de Bry, venales reperiūtur in officina S. Feirabēdii, 1591 [plate] 5. G159 .B7 Rosenwald Coll. Rare Book and Special Collections Division, Library of Congress. Copy negative number LC-USZ62-380 in Prints and Photographs Division, Library of Congress.

Page 19 Wie der Floridaner Stätte erbauweisenen. Illus. in: Americae, Theodor de Bry, ed. München: Konrad Kölbl, 1970 reprint of edition published 1600, part II, pl. XXX. Prints and Photographs Division, Library of Congress. E141.B88 1970. Copy negative number LC-USZ62-100255.

Pages 20–21 Vinckeboons, Joan. Map of the Peninsula of Florida, 1639? G3291.S12 coll .H3 Vault: Harr vol. 2, map 11.

Pages 22–23 Sanson, Nicolas. La Floride, par N. Sanson d'Abbeville, Georgr. ordre. du Roÿ. A Paris chez l'Auteur aux Galleries du Louvre. Avec Pri. pour 20 ans. Paris, 1657. G3860 1657 .S3 Vault: Low 149.

Pages 24–25 Lajonk, Jaime. Descripcion de la Bahia de Santa Maria de Galve, y Puerto de Sn. Miguel de Panzacola con toda la costa contigua y las demas bahias que tiene en ella, hasta el Rio de Apalache, observada, y reconozida por los ingenieros Dn. Jaime Lajonk, y Don Juan de Siscara, 1700. G3932.F555P5 1700 .L3 Vault: Vellum 22.

Notes

Pages 26–27 Crisp, Edward. A compleat description of the province of Carolina in 3 parts: 1st, the improved part from the surveys of Maurice Mathews & Mr. John Love: 2ly, the west part by Capt. Tho. Nairn: 3ly, a chart of the coast from Virginia to Cape Florida, published by Edw. Crisp; engraved by John Harris. London, 1711? G3870 1711 .C6 Vault Oversize.

Pages 32–33 (detail, page 28) L'Isle, Guillaume de. Carta geografica dell' America settentrionale. Venezia, 1750. G3300 1750 .L4 Low 396.

Pages 34–35 López de Vargas Machuca, Tomás. Mapa maritimo del Golfo de Mexico e islas de la America, para el uso de los navegantes en esta parte del mundo, construido sobre las mexores memorias, y observaciones astronomicas de longitudes, y latitudes. Dedicado a la Catholica Magestad de Don Fernando VI Rey de España, y de las Yndias, por sus mas rendidos, y fieles vasallos, Thomas Lopez, y Juan de la Cruz. Madrid, 1755. G4391.P5 1755 .L6 Low 417.

Pages 36–37 Jefferys, Thomas. Plan of Amelia Island in East Florida, north point of Amelia Island lyes in 30:55 north latitude 80:23 w. longitude from London, taken from De Brahm's Map of South Caroline & Georgia. A chart of the entrance into St. Mary's River, taken by W. Fuller in November 1769. A c[hart] of the [mouth of] Nassau River with the bar and the soundings on it, taken at low water by W. Fuller. To the Right Honourable John Earl of Egmont &c. this plate is most humbly inscribed by his lordship's most obedient humble servant, Willm. Fuller. London, 1770. G3932.A4 1770 .J4 Vault.

Pages 38–39 Map showing Caribbean area including West Indies and Gulf of Mexico, ca. 1770. G4390 1770 .M3 Vellum 33.

Pages 40–41 Taitt, David. A plan of part of the rivers Tombecbe, Alabama, Tensa, Perdido, & Scambia in the province of West Florida; with a sketch of the boundary between the nation of upper Creek Indians and that part of the province which is contiguous thereto, as settled at the congresses at Pensacola in the years 1765 & 1771. Collected from different surveys at the desire of the Hon'ble John Stuart, Esquire, sole agent and superintendant of Indian Affairs for the southern district of North America, 1771? G3971.P53 1771 .T3 Vault.

Pages 42–43 Durnford, Elias Walker. Thomas Hutchins' land grant and map to 2000 acres in West Florida, by Elias Durnford, Surveyor General, 1776. G4014. B3G465 1776 .D8 Vault.

Pages 44–45 Romans, Bernard. A general map of the southern British colonies in America, comprehending North and South Carolina, Georgia, East and West Florida, with the neighboring Indian countries, from the modern surveys of Engineer de Brahm, Capt. Collet, Mouzon, & others, and from the large hydrographical survey of the coasts of East and West Florida. London, Printed for R. Sayer and J. Bennett, map, chart, and printsellers, 1776. G3870 1776 .R6 Vault: Low 585.

Pages 46–47 Purcell, Joseph. A plan of Pensacola and its environs in its present state, from an actual survey in 1778, pub.1778. G3934.P4 1778 .P8 Vault.

Pages 48–49 Romans, Bernard. Maps of East and West Florida. B. Romans, inv. delin. & in Ære incidit. New York, 1781. G3861.P5 s500 .R6 Vault.

Pages 50–51 López de Vargas Machuca, Tomás. Plano de la ciudad y puerto de San Agustin de la Florida. Madrid, 1783. G3934.S2 1783 .L6 Vault.

Pages 52–53 Bahia de Tampa Madrid, Dericción de Hidrografia, 1809. G3932.T3 1809 .S7 TIL.

Pages 54–55 Hackley, Richard S. Map of the lands belonging to R.S. Hackley, esq., in east Florida, 1823? G3931. G46 1823 .H3 Vault.

Pages 56–57 Melish, John Græme. Geographical conversation cards: states of the United States, invented and drawn by John Græme Melish. New York: A.T. Goodrich, 1824 (Clayton & Van Norden, printers). G3701.A9 svar .M4 Vault Shelf.

Pages 58–59 Map of the territory of Florida, from its northern boundary to lat. 27°30′N, connected with the delta of the Mississippi: annexed to the report of the Board of Internal Improvement dated Febr. 19th, 1829, relating to the canal contemplated to connect the Atlantic with the Gulf of Mexico and describing the inland navigation parallel to the coast from the Mississippi to the Bay of Espiritu Santo and from St. Mary's Harbour to St. Augustine this map has been compiled under the direction of the Board of Internal Improvement ... ; drawn and compiled by W.H. Swift, lt. artillery. Washington, D.C.?: Board of Internal Improvement, 1829. G3860 1829 .U5 Oversize

Page 60 Map of a part of west-Florida, [18--]. G3932.A72 18-- .M3 Vault: Jackson 1.

Page 61 Seat of War. United States Army Corps of Engineers, 1839. G3931.E1 1839 .U5 TIL.

Page 62 Key West harbor and its approaches. From a trigonometrical survey under the direction of A. D. Bache, Superintendent of the survey of the coast of the United States. Triangulation by J. E. Hilgard, Assistant. Topography by L. H. Adams, Sub-Asst. Hydrography by the party under the command of Lieut. John Rodgers, U.S. Navy Assistant. Redd. drng. by E. K. Knorr. Engd. by E. Yeager, E. F. Woodward, and H. M. Knight. Washington: U.S. Coast Survey, 1864. G3934.K6 1864 .U5 CW 117.7.

Pages 66–67 Sketch showing the positions of the beacons on the Florida reefs erected by Lieut. James Totten, U.S. Army, Assistant, U.S.C.S. Washington: U.S. Coast Survey, 1861. G3932.F5 1861 .U5 CW 117.6.

Pages 68–69 Bachmann, John. Birds eye view of Florida and part of Georgia and Alabama Drawn from nature and lith. by John Bachmann. New York: John Bachmann, c1861. G3931.A35 1861 .B3 CW 117.2.

Pages 70–71 Preliminary chart of Escambia and Santa Maria de Galvaez [i.e., East] Bays, Florida. From a trigonometrical survey under the direction of A. D. Bache, Superintendent of the survey of the coast of the United States. Triangulation and topography by F. H. Gerdes, Asst. Hydrography by the party under the command of Lieut. Comdg. T. S. Phelps. U.S.N. Assist. Washington: U.S. Coast Survey, 1861. G3932.E69 1861 .U5 CW 117.4.

Pages 72–73 Colton, Joseph Hutchins. Colton's plans of U. S. harbors showing the position & vicinities of the most important fortifications on the sea-board and in the interior From U.S. surveys and other authentic sources. New York: Printed by Lang & Laing, 1862. G3701.P55 1862 .C6 CW 26.

Page 74 St. Mary's River and Fernandina harbor, Florida From a trigonometrical survey under the direction of A. D. Bache, Superintendent of the survey of the coast of the United States. Triangulation by Capt. J. H. Simpson and Lieutenant A. W. Evans, U.S.A. Assistants. Topography by A. M. Harrison, Assistant. Hydrography by the party under the command of Lieut. S. D. Trenchard, U.S.N. Assist. 1857. Resurvey of bar by C. O. Boutelle, Asst. in 1862. Redd. drng. by P. Witzel. Engd. by A. Maedel and R. F. Bartle. Bowen & Co. lith., Philada. Washington: U.S. Coast Survey, 1862. G3922.S18 1862 .U5 CW 120.5.

Page 75 Williams, W. A. Sketch of Pensacola Navy Yard and Fort Pickens from U.S. coast surveys. By W. A. Williams, Civil Engineer. Boston: L. Prang & Co., 186-. G3934. P4:2P4 186- .W5 CW 120.

Pages 76–77 Steinwehr, Adolph Von. Map showing the distribution of slaves in the Southern States, projected & compiled by A. von Steinwehr. Philadelphia, Pa.?, 186-. G3861.E9 186- .S7 Vault.

Page 78 Drew, C[olumbus]. Drew's new map of the state of Florida, showing the townships by the U.S. Surveys, the completed & projected railroads, the different railroad stations and growing railroad towns. The new towns on the rivers and interior, and the new counties, up to the year 1874. Jacksonville, pub. 1874, c1873. G3931.P3 1874 .D7 RR 195.

Pages 82–83 Maps showing the Florida Transit and Peninsula Rail Road and its connections. New York: G.W. & C.B. Colton & Co., 1882. G3931.P3 1882 .G15 RR 408.

Page 84 Coral distribution in 1881 at Dry Tortugas, Florida, after Agassiz (1883). Florida?, pub. 1979? G3932. D7D1 1881 .C6.

Page 85 Stoner, J. J. Bird's eye view of Key West, Fla., Key West Island, C.S. Monroe Co., 1884, Wellge del. Madison, Wis., 1884. (Milwaukee: Beck & Pauli, litho.). G3934.K6A3 1884 .S8.

Pages 86–87 Green Cove Springs, county seat of Clay County, Florida. 1885. Beck & Pauli, litho. Milwaukee: Norris, Wellge & Co., c1885. G3934.G6A3 1885 .N6.

Pages 88–89 Koch, Augustus, Jacksonville, Florida. Drawn, published and copyrighted by August Koch. [K[ansas] C[ity] Mo.: Hudson-Kimberly Pub. Co., 1893. G3934. J2A3 1893 .K6.

Pages 90–91 Correct map of Florida: season of 1894-5: showing the Tropical Trunk Line: comprising the Jacksonville, Tampa & Key West R'y, the Florida Southern Railroad Co., Indian River Steamboat Company, Jupiter & Lake Worth Railway, Lake Worth steamers, and connections: leading from Jacksonville to the east coast, the west coast, the south coast. Buffalo, N.Y.: Matthews-Northrup Co., 1894. G3931.P3 1894 .M3.

Page 92 Beckwith, J. P. The east coast of Florida is paradise regained, 1898. G3931.P3 1898 .B4 TIL.

Pages 96–97 Pleuthner, W. K. Panoramic view of West Palm Beach, North Palm Beach and Lake Worth, 1915. G3933.P2 1915 .P5 TIL.

Pages 98–99 Map of the City of Miami and Environs Showing The Greater Miami Development and the Estimated Expansion for 1935. Compiled and drawn by Sauer and Seghy, 1936.

Pages 100–101 Wynne, James. Aero-view of Tallahassee, 1926. G3934.T2A3 1926 .W9.

Pages 102–3 (detail, page 110) Map Showing World Famous Resorts on the East Coast of Florida. Buffalo, NY: J.W. Clement Co.-Matthews-Northrup Works, 1929.

Pages 104–5 Orlando—"Florida's City Beautiful" Official City Map. Orlando, Florida: Greater Orlando Chamber of Commerce, 1936.

Pages 106–7 Florida, prepared by Geography Division in cooperation with Data Preparation Division. Washington, D.C.: U.S. Dept. of Commerce, Bureau of the Census, 1983. G3931.F7 1980 .U5.

Pages 108–9 Central America and the Caribbean. Washington, D.C.: Central Intelligence Agency, 1990. G4800 1990 .U5.

About the Authors

VINCENT VIRGA earned critical praise for *Cartographia: Mapping Civilization*, and he coauthored *Eyes of the Nation: A Visual History of the United States* with the Library of Congress and Alan Brinkley. Among his other books are *The Eighties: Images of America*, with a foreword by Richard Rhodes; *Eisenhower: A Centennial Life*, with text by Michael Beschloss; and *The American Civil War: 365 Days*, with Gary Gallagher and Margaret Wagner. He has been hailed as "America's foremost picture editor" for having researched, edited, and designed nearly 150 picture sections in books by authors who include John Wayne, Jane Fonda, Arianna Huffington, Walter Cronkite, Hillary Clinton, and Bill Clinton. Virga edited *Forcing Nature: Trees in Los Angeles*, photographs by George Haas for Vincent Virga Editions. He is the author of six novels, including *Gaywyck*, *Vadriel Vail*, and *A Comfortable Corner*, as well as publisher of ViVa Editions. He has a Web site through the Author's Guild at www.vincentvirga.com.

E. LYNNE WRIGHT, a Pennsylvanian now residing in Vero Beach, Florida, a lover of books and history, was a nurse anesthetist, wife, and mother of three before embarking on a writing career. Since then, her short stories, nonfiction articles, essays, and book reviews have appeared in the *Cleveland Plain Dealer*, *Hartford Courant*, *Mature Lifestyles*, *Woman's Day*, and numerous anthologies and literary magazines. Exploring Florida by land and boat has inspired a love for the state's natural beauty, its people, and its history. Lynne is also the author of *More than Petticoats: Remarkable Florida Women*, *Disasters and Heroic Rescues of Florida*, and *It Happened in Florida*.